PLUCK UNDER FIRE

First edition, published in 2001 by

WOODFIELD PUBLISHING
Woodfield House, Babsham Lane, Bognor Regis
West Sussex PO21 5EL, England.

ISBN 1-903953-08-1

ISBN 1 - 903953- 08- 1

9 781903 953082

Pluck Under Fire

My Korean War experiences with
The Middlesex Regiment 1950/51

JOHN PLUCK

Woodfield Publishing
~ WEST SUSSEX · ENGLAND ~

Private Hissey with a headless Chinese corpse – Korea 1951.

*This book is dedicated
to the memory of Private Hissey
— a man of true courage and loyalty.*

The Author

John Pluck was born on 2nd August 1927.

He served in the British Army for
twenty-two and a half years.

He died on a date yet to be announced...

*The Author, on the 7th consecutive day of combat
during the Battle of Billingsgate, Korea, April 1951.*

List of Chapters

CHAPTER ONE

Not Yet a Man

In September 1950 I was twenty three years of age, a Corporal of the Infantry and, without doubt, one of the most highly battle trained soldiers of the British Army. I had been a Weapons Instructor for nearly five years, had passed the Senior Instructors' Course at the Small Arms School, and the School of Infantry. My achievements, however, had always been overshadowed by one large dark cloud. I had no experience of actual battle in any war, large or small. True, I was not alone in this respect. By some quirk of nature, it had been discovered that the best instructors of eighteen year old recruits were old soldiers of eighteen and a half.

And so, along with thousands of others, I was a recruit one day and a Lance Corporal the next. Promotion to Full Corporal came just four months later, and promotion to Acting Sergeant came fifteen months after that on my twentieth birthday. Eight months on, my unit was disbanded. I was back to Corporal looking at a long waiting list for another chance of three stripes.

In addition to my personal trials and tribulations, the Corps of Infantry had undergone a vast change in structure after 1945. Since the 1870s all infantry regiments had been formed into two Regular Units, i.e. The 1st and 2nd Battalions of the 35th of Foot, The Royal Sussex Regiment. During the World Wars, the regimental strength was increased by the mobilisation of the Territorial Army battalions such as the 4th, the 5th, etc. Come 1945 and the Territorial Army units reverted to their peace time roles, but the Regular Army regiments were in for a shock. By 1948, the 2nd Battalion of each infantry regiment had been disbanded, supposedly as a temporary measure. Hindsight shows that these 2nd battalions were never brought back to life. Quite simply, the New Army did not require so many infantry soldiers. (I do not include the Brigade of Guards in this explanation.)

Ironically, the new titles of each infantry regiment never reverted to the pre 1870 condition. It was never the 35th of Foot, the Royal Sussex, but always the First battalion, the Royal Sussex Regiment. A decade later and even that system was on the way out, but that is another story.

The new structure was not, of course, without its problems. Prior to 1939 each infantry regiment had its two battalions and a Depot where recruits were given their initial training. Generally speaking, it was the usual practise to have one battalion at home and one away, i.e. abroad. The recruits on completion of training were normally posted to whichever battalion was in a home station. When the away battalion needed to be made up to strength, a draft was dispatched from the home battalion. Come 1948 and only one battalion to the regiment, there arose a need to find reinforcements for overseas units which did not consist of a draft of raw recruits. The problem was solved by amalgamating a number of regiments into a paper brigade. For instance, The Royal Sussex, The Buffs, The Queen's Regiment, The East Surreys, The Royal West Kents, The Middlesex Regiment and The Royal Fusiliers were formed into the Home Counties Brigade. The Headquarters and Infantry Training Unit was at Shornecliffe, Kent. Each Regiment took it in turn to act as a cadre of instructors to the recruits. In September 1950 it was the turn of The Royal West Kents.

The preceding paragraph may give the impression that recruits, on completion of training, were never sent out on overseas postings without a period of acclimatisation at home first. This may have been the original intention by the War Office, but when needs must, the Devil drives. This was also the heyday of the National Serviceman and, when the only reinforcements are National Service recruits, then the National Service boys were sent out in large numbers to all corners of the Empire. But more of that later.

In April 1948, after three years service, I was posted to the 1st Battalion, The Royal Fusiliers, then stationed at Iserlohn, Germany. The next two years were quite eventful with training on a massive scale, with mock wars involving British, French, Belgium and American forces – all good stuff in preparation for the real war in Korea. In November 1949 my regiment took over duties of occupation troops at Spandau, Berlin.

The reader of this book may be feeling a little impatient with not yet having read about the Korean War, but I beg of you to remain calm. The following paragraphs are required reading to explain the attitude of the British Government and the British Officers towards the Korean conflict. They may also explain some very peculiar decisions made by the Brigade and Regimental Officers in the first months of the Korean War. They will certainly explain my attitude to battle and some peculiar decisions made by myself along the way.

Still in September 1950 and my morale was at a low ebb. In June 1950 I had been sent on a parachute course at Aldershot, but had failed the first part, which was all physical training. Deeply disappointed though I was, the failure was not all that surprising. I had been born prematurely and my life was held in suspense for six months. I grew up small and very light in weight, but somehow kept up with the other children in their play and rough games. Indeed, I was often the unwitting leader in some respects. I was very aware of the public worship of heroes such as explorers and fearless conquerors of savage tribes, and I was in no doubt that I was cast in the same mould.

Fortunately for me, my Father was a Regular Soldier and the family occupied Married Quarters at various Military establishments. In order of memory, from five years of age to thirteen, there was Bulford Camp, Mill Hill, Catterick Camp, Aldershot, Tidworth and Bulford Camp again. With the exception of Mill Hill, all of these places were set in vast acres of uncultivated land. The only inhabitants were Zulus, Pathans and Red Indians. When school and Mam allowed, I would set off for the far distant horizon, quelling the restless natives along the way. Usually, I would walk until I was fit to drop and, only then, realise I had to walk all the way back again. Still, it satisfied my yearnings for exploration, a yearning that has never left me.

I cannot move away from September 1950 without making a confession. A confession which is vital in understanding my motive for wanting to be seen as a proper leader of men. At that time, I was a sexual virgin, never having known the most tender caresses a woman can bestow. Never, never, would I have made such a confession at the age of twenty three, and it is only now that I can make the admission with pride. I was to lose my virginity only five months later, but I never ever felt the urge to boast about the loss, and I never really felt any difference in myself, except for an overwhelming sense of relief. I had already proven myself in battle and, in February 1951, I was a man complete.

For further understanding of what makes men volunteer for combat, we must disect the minds of any given group of about one hundred recruits of eighteen and nineteen years of age. Of this one hundred, ninety eight will continually boast about their sexual conquests. This same ninety eight would be blatant liars but frantic to prove their manhood among their equals. Of the two remaining, one will be sexually experienced but no longer with a need to boast about some imagined happening. He will let the lunatic ravings wash over and go past him. The other would be a person like me. Terrified of being found out but without the urge to lie. He would just stumble through it all and generally do without the company of the canteen cowboys.

Of this same one hundred young men, when faced with a prospect of combat, about ninety will snap at the chance to prove their worth as men in one way, if not the other. Instinctively, they also knew that combat experience will increase their likelihood of conquering that elusive Everest known as carnal desire. The risk of being killed or maimed is totally disregarded when weighed against the very real opportunity of becoming a complete human. Tales, with much embellishment, will have been handed down about the available maidens desperate to reward the soldier for just a few pence. Maidens moreover who will not jeer at fumblings and embarrassment. Too good an opportunity to turn down lightly. One of those ninety would have been me, but at my age then of twenty three, I had other more pressing reasons to volunteer for combat. Of the remaining ten, eight will not take active steps to avoid going overseas, but will be grateful for any mishap that will prevent them being sent to a corner of a foreign field. Two will do virtually anything to avoid the danger but, at the same time, these two must not be seen acting in a manner that is tantamount to conduct unbecoming. So, in effect, these two will just go along with the rest anyway. Of these dubious ten, only very rarely will any of them face a court martial or other Courts of Justice. Along with the other survivors, these ten will also return as heroes. And why not?

Before I proceed any further, I must explain one huge advantage I had over my fellow soldiers in Korea. Apart from being very highly trained, I was a natural born sharpshooter. From the first time I fired some .22 calibre rounds at the indoor range, it was obvious that I was a very competent marksman. I can say this without any vanity on my part, as subsequent years gained me many trophies at Bisley and elsewhere. As I write, I have a case on my wall filled with medals and spoons from my shooting career. More importantly, several cups and other trophies had been awarded me **before** I served in Korea. Let's face it! Even with training and practise, most soldiers still can't hit the side of a barn. My noted skill with firearms gave me an enormous amount of confidence in battle, and on at least three occasions in Korea my ability with weapons saved my life and the lives of others. I now thank those officers, especially of The Royal Fusiliers, who encouraged me to take up competition shooting.

CHAPTER TWO

Still to Hear a Shot Fired in Anger

When the year 1965 had gone past, it was announced by the Ministry of Defence that 1965 was the only year in the twentieth century in which no serviceman or woman had been killed by enemy action. This record still stood until at least 1996 and perhaps later. For the average civilian, and for a large number of servicemen, War was defined as those periods of 1914-1918 and 1939-1945. Otherwise it was peacetime.

This sort of thinking is no consolation to those killed in action during skirmishes in places such as Ashanti in West Africa, the Nandi Wars in East Africa, Russia 1919-1920, Sudan in the 1920s and especially the North West Frontier of India, where warfare was a continual occupation for native tribes. Not surprisingly, the invasion of South Korea by North Korea in June 1950 did not at first cause much of a stir in British Empire political circles. But a rude awakening came via the United States of America. Britain and literally scores of other Western nations were sharply reminded that we were all part of the United Nations, an organisation formed for the express purpose of suppressing warfare among its member states. Even so, perhaps the invasion would still go largely unremarked except for the presence in South Korea of an occupation force composed entirely of Americans. The Americans, as such, were fanatically opposed to Communism, and here were peace loving Yanks being slaughtered by the Commies. Something had to be done, and so the call for support went out far and wide.

Most of the larger nations of the Western world had standing armies which could have supplied the first support to the U.S. but by sheer chance, or rather by courtesy of the British Empire, the nearest fighting troops were British. Two infantry regiments, The Middlesex and The Argyle and Sutherland Highlanders were stationed in Hong Kong, and the 3rd Royal Australian Regiment was part of the occupying force in Japan. The two British battalions landed at Pusan in the far south on the 28th August 1950 and were followed on the 28th September by the Australians.

I don't want to impose or detract from other authors, and so I will not attempt to describe the actions that involved the first British troops in Korea covering the period 28th August to 28th September 1950 for the simple reason, I was not there. There is one incident, however, that needs some explaining if only to show how the media will distort the facts for a good story, and co-incidentally hammer the Government along the way. On the 8th September 1950, Private R. Streeter was killed returning from a patrol. He was the first of The Middlesex Regiment to die but even his death was wildly misreported at the time, and for another forty years after. Supposedly, the Private was a driver of a Jeep carrying a Major on a reconnaissance. Apparently, the Jeep was ambushed and both Private and Major killed. However, the Roll of Honour of the Regiment does not list any Killed in Action higher than a Lieutenant. At first, Private Streeter was listed as Missing, which gave the Press a field day for a week in spite of Private Streeter being buried in a Military Cemetery on the day after his death. "Missing" is still the rather more romantic role of a casualty in battle and inevitably the myth still persists. A full forty years after the truce was signed, I read an account of the experiences of one of our Prisoners-of-War. The ex-Prisoner stated that one morning, when queuing for food, he saw a strange face – one that belonged to a squaddy who was rather silent and sad. On enquiries being made, the stranger said, "My name is Streeter and I have been a prisoner since September 1950." Perhaps there is a mystery about Streeter's death, but there was something that made this Private Soldier's demise very, very important. Streeter was a National Serviceman.

In the year 1990 I found out from my research that the British Government had given instructions to all the very senior officers that British units in Korea were to avoid the real shooting war if at all possible. After six years of World War Two, the public did not want to hear of more deaths by enemy action. Parliament could get away with casualties in Palestine and India, and the Arabian Peninsula as these conflicts were virtually everlasting. Korea, however, was something different. Not really any of our business. In addition, when National Service was established, it was generally understood that National Servicemen would only be sent to the safe places. A promise that was impossible to keep from the word go. We simply did not have the Regulars to satisfy the overseas demands. And so, the death of Private Streeter was the sensation of the day.

But back to the camp at Shornecliffe, and especially the Holding and Drafting Company which had me kicking my heels waiting to return to The Royal Fusiliers in Germany. On or about the 10th September 1950 there appeared in the camp some one hundred and forty Officers, NCOs and men from The Queen's Regiment stationed in Germany. They were the first reinforcements to be sent to The Middlesex Regiment. It was all hustle and bustle with numerous inoculations and the issue of tropical kit. After two days had elapsed, I went to see the Second-in-Command of the Drafting Company. This Captain was about six foot four tall and he was standing at the top of four steps leading up to his office. His head was a long way from my five foot four, but I spoke up.

"Would it be possible for me to join that draft going to Korea, Sir?".

The Captain peered down at me, sneered and said, "We don't need you. Besides, it will all be over by Christmas."

I saluted and went away with my morale even lower than before. I rather think the Captain had been waiting for years to use that expression about Christmas, and the time was appropriate. As in August 1914 and September 1939, he was proved to be wrong, of course, but come Christmas 1950 I was in the mood to wish he had been right.

On that same day, the draft was sent home on a weeks leave. Four days later, at 9 am, I was walking back to my billet, having just completed a tour of duty as Orderly Corporal of the Day. I was entitled to the rest of the day off. My journey took me past a row of Nissen Huts. These huts were bounded by two roads and I was on one of them. Looking through the gap between two huts, I saw my Company Commander, a Major, the Company Sergeant Major and the Orderly Room Sergeant proceeding in the opposite direction to myself. I whipped up a salute to the Major and my hand froze at my head. A huge bellow had come from the Sergeant.

"There he is!" and all three of them came running towards me, actually running. I stood to attention wildly trying to think of what I had done wrong.

The trio halted and the Major was actually smiling.

"Do you still want to go to Korea?" the Major asked, although I rather felt I no longer had a choice.

"Yes, I do, Sir."

"Good man" said the Major. "Come back to the Company Lines and we will get you kitted out and whatnot."

Back at the Drafting Company lines, I was the sole object of attention of a dozen assorted Officers and NCOs, none of whom were being sent to Korea. I was marched to the Medical Inspection Room to be vaccinated and had injections of Yellow Fever, Cholera, and a couple of other now forgotten diseases. I was issued with Khaki Drill for the tropics, and made a special trip to the tailors for a fitting. Every department had orders to attend to my every Military need, without question. Before going to my bed that night, I had found out the reason for my sudden induction on the draft. On arrival at Shornecliffe, several Corporals had suddenly remembered they had bad backs; a condition that had been present since childbirth but gallantly concealed in the comparative safety of Germany. The prospect of a real shooting war provoked a rash of physical afflictions. Strangely enough, these Corporals all appeared to be married to Germans and living in Married Quarters in the Rhineland.

The next day there was another round of inoculations and adjustments of clothing, etc. I only knew where Korea was from reading the papers. Actually, Korea was a country unknown to the British Army. The occupation forces were American and Australian, and even the Australians had withdrawn from the country by 1946. In light of the lack of knowledge of conditions in Korea, it was decided by the authorities that we humble soldiers would retain all our Home Service kit and carry the Tropical kit as well. Never have so many kitbags been stuffed with so much for such futile reasoning.

Because our immediate travelling conditions and subsequent living conditions in the war zone were at the discretion of the Quartermaster and his crew, I will take this opportunity to air my gripes about Quartermasters in general. For any sailors reading this, I am aware that Quartermasters in the Royal Navy are chaps who steer the ship (I think). In the Army, a Quartermaster is an old soldier awarded an inferior commission and who looks after clothing equipment, stores and accommodation. He is assisted by a Warrant Officer Class Two who is the Regimental Quartermaster Sergeant, the senior in the regiment below the Regimental Sergeant Major. Each rifle company and Headquarters Company have a Company Sergeant Major who is responsible for discipline and, below him, is a Company Quartermaster Sergeant who is responsible for stores, etc. This chap wears three stripes and a crown and is called the Colour Sergeant. Until 1911 the Colour Sergeant was the Senior Non-Commissioned Officer in the Company. From 1911 the Company Sergeant Major came into being and was graded a Warrant Officer Class Two.

Anyway, over the centuries there has crept in a type of thinking (by the Generals) that each and every soldier must at all times be furnished with every item of clothing and equipment that he needs now and may have to use in the foreseeable future. Not only that, but allowance is made for washing items and putting stuff through the laundry; and so, three shirts, four pairs of socks, two pairs of boots and so on. Neither was the rule of three ever abated. One on, one in the wash, and one for inspection. Going along with this type of thinking was that other rule. No soldier must have in his possession any item in excess of that laid down in regulations. Along with this criteria was that other regulation regarding food. One ration per man per day – not an ounce more or less. But more of that in Korea!

CHAPTER THREE

Still Preparing for that First Shot

On my second day, a Friday, of frantic rush, I was given a rail warrant for the purpose of leave from 6 p.m. that day until 10 p.m. on the Sunday.

"Sorry we can't give you any more," said the Major, but I was highly delighted to be going to a war zone anyway. My joy though was in for a rude shock. When I had my last inoculation of six over two days, the Medical Officer, a youngish Captain, said, "I may not be able to pass you fit to leave on Monday. All these inoculations are a terrific thump to your body. When do you come back from leave?"

His eyes were shining bright when he spoke and he seemed nervous and on edge.

"I have to be back at ten o'clock Sunday night, Sir," I told him

"Well then," he said. "I'll tell you what... I'm on duty at the Camp Hospital. Come and see me at Casualty when you get back." I duly reported to the Hospital at 10.15 p.m. on Sunday and told the Orderly why I was there. I sat there for an hour until the Captain popped his head round a curtain.

"All right, you can go," he snapped. There was no examination of any kind. Ever since that day I have wondered about the Captain's real motive in summoning me to that hospital.

My home, a very poor one, was near Leicester but contained only my elderly Mother, a sister and brother. My Father lived alone in Leeds and was trying to get a home for all of us to live together. Conditions were so bad that I sometimes went home on leave with reluctance. In any event, I went to see the family with the good news. I had an older stepsister and stepbrother who lived nearby and somehow my Father was contacted and he came down from Leeds on the Sunday. There was drinking in the pub on Saturday night and on the Sunday lunchtime but not to excess. I was never a drinking man anyway. My Mother cried when I left, but she had seen two husbands and five sons going off to war from 1914 until she died in 1973. Except for the years 1917-1918 there was never a time when at least a husband or one son was not in the Armed Forces. For the last six months of World War Two there were five of us in the Army at the same time. Counting my Mother's first husband, there were seven of us with at least thirty campaign medals between us by the 1950s and those medals covered about twenty one separate tours of service in various campaigns starting with the Boer War.

The reader can see that I had a lot of tradition to live up to, but there is even more. My Mother's Father served in the Leicestershire Regiment from about 1863 until 1893 with the last eighteen years in India. Many male descendants of this old Tiger served in the Army down to a great grandson in the 1980s. My Father's side of the family were equally endowed with Regular Soldiers for a lengthy period of history. But they were Irish from County Mayo and so loyalty to the British

Crown existed from 1922 only through my Father and one of his brothers.

On the Monday morning following my leave, I fell in with the draft from the Queen's Regiment and we moved off to an airfield near Aldershot that same day. On arrival it was discovered that we had to undergo yet another inoculation before we could board the aircraft. I don't know about the others, but for me this particular jab raised a small painful lump on my left arm within minutes. Several days later the pain had gone but the lump remained. Over the next forty eight years that lump just got bigger and bigger until now it is quite noticeable. I suppose I will have to mention it to a doctor sometime.

On that first day with my new comrades, I could not help noticing, or mostly hearing, a tall well-built chap who was all mouth. Cruel jokes were thrown out from his coarse face and mainly at the expense of the Officers and Sergeants.

"Go on, Charlie. You tell 'em!" yelled his clique of hangers on. Most of the draft ignored him or showed their disgust. After that first day the voice got quieter, and by the time we landed in Korea it was non-existent. I only remember seeing him just once in the early days of the campaign and he was not spouting off as usual. Looking rather sick, in fact, as we had our first sight of the enemy dead from battles with the Yanks. For the life of me, I just can't place his face anywhere during the following eight months. I suppose he was hived off to some batman's job well to the rear.

In the normal coarse of events, when one Regiment is asked to supply a draft for another Regiment, it is well recognised as a glorious opportunity to get rid of the worst of a bad lot. True, in this draft from the Queen's, there were some complete wasters, especially among the Corporals. On the other hand, the Officers and Sergeants appeared to be of the best. The bulk of the men were average and I suppose that this particular draft represented a true cross section of the Queen's Regiment.

Generally speaking from 1939 until the end of National Service in 1961 the average infantry soldier came rather low in general ability. The volunteer, of course, is exempt from this condemnation. For those who waited for call up during the period of emergency and for the National Serviceman, the choice of which arm of the Army the soldier was assigned to was at the discretion of the Personnel Selection Officer. The P.S.O. had many calls upon his services and had to direct the better educated and more mentally efficient to those areas where the man's talents could be properly utilised. The Royal Corps of Signals and the Royal Engineers were just two of the Corps which required the best. Only two arms of the service came below the Infantry in order of competence and they were the Royal Pioneer Corps and the Army Catering Corps. Anybody can learn to dig a hole or to cook or to be an Infantry soldier, but the Infantryman also had to be physically fit. There were a number of exceptions to this rule, of course, and I was to meet all kinds in the following years.

Apart from the volunteer Regular soldier and the National Serviceman, who was determined to do only his allotted term, there were two other types of soldier I must mention. One was the young civilian bad lad who was frequently up before the beak. Finally, and in exasperation, the Magistrate gave the offender a choice.

"Three years in the Army or three years in Borstal."

If the young man had any sense he chose, of course, the Army and usually this choice implied Infantry soldiering. Some of this type never changed their bad habits and were frequently in the cells. Some turned out to be very good soldiers and, quite often, extended their terms of engagement. Most just got through their three years keeping a low profile. The other type was the three year volunteer. The Army brought in a recruitment dodge that was quite effective. After call up the National Serviceman could change to a three year engagement instead of his two year compulsory enlistment. There were benefits, of course. A total of one hundred and twelve days leave instead of just twenty one days for the National Service chap. More importantly, the three year man got a further twenty one shillings a week, virtually doubling his income. For the young man who had left a dead end job with no prospects, this was a golden opportunity. A fair number took the plunge. Even in 1950 there was very little chance of seeing active service and if the soldier was already in Germany, it was more than likely that his three years would be a fairly safe bet. But then, nobody anticipated the Korean War!

This then was the make up of the men awaiting to make the flight to Korea. Some bad, some good, most just average and split between three year Regulars and National Service. I am not sure about the two senior officers or the Company Sergeant Major with the draft, but I'm fairly certain nobody else had been up in a plane before. Later, in Hong Kong, after Korea, an ex-paratrooper joined my company, but he was another big mouth who I can't place in Korea. Anyway, we were split up into four plane loads for the flight to Japan. Each aircraft was a converted Hastings bomber. Just over thirty men were allocated to each plane. My particular contingent was commanded by a tall, well-built, handsome Lieutenant who looked every inch a soldier. I rather thought I would like to be in his Platoon when we were sorted out. As it turned out, I was. There was also a Sergeant in this plane load but he went to a different setup in Korea.

There must have been two or three other Corporals with this flight, but if any responsibility was delegated it came to me. However, on the first flight to Malta I was very sick. It wasn't air sickness though. I had known travel sickness all my life. Trains, buses, cars, it was all the same. If the journey was too long or too hot, I was ill. This sickness came upon me about two hours in on a seven hour flight to Malta, and it was hardly surprising considering the number of jabs I had been given in such a short space of time. I had a headache and I was sweating buckets. I had got over my very first take off in a plane and was looking forward to the touchdown. That I don't remember at all. I can't even remember getting off the plane. When I was on firm ground at the R.A.F. airport, I asked where the Medical Officer was situated. I was put on the right track, but it was now about seven o'clock in the evening, having flown East. I saw some Medical Orderlies who immediately assumed I was trying to work my passage back home. However, I was given a couple of Aspirin and bedded down for the night in their small hospital. The next morning the fever was gone and I rejoined my comrades for breakfast in the dining hall. The conversation consisted of tales of the fabulous night out they all had down some place called the Gut.

The booze and the girls were fabulous but I did wonder how they paid for it all. Apparently, some of the more enterprising had sold their boots and this may be true. We all had to carry our plimsolls as hand luggage and change into them before getting on the plane. When we landed we changed back into boots.

The next stage of the journey was to another R.A.F. airfield in Iraq. The local natives had been rather restless that week and we were all confined to camp. We had a mediocre meal, but were allowed to go to the N.A.A.F.I. canteen. On then, the next day, to Karachi in Pakistan. It was there that I had yet another set back to my ambition to fight in Korea. The medical people in Pakistan were red hot on certificates for all the required inoculations; in particular, the Yellow Fever one. It had to be not less than two weeks old. All the rest of the draft were O.K. My certificate was only seven days in age. There was going around the story of a Brigadier who had landed the day before. His certificate also was only a week old. He was promptly removed from the flight and put in quarantine until his jab had matured for the right length of time. I reasoned that if they could do that to a Brigadier, what chance did I have! Desperate measures were required. With a razor blade I scratched out the typed date and replaced it with the earlier one, but in ink.

One hundred and twenty of us were queuing up to have our certificates passed by a Major of the Pakistan Army. I pushed myself into the middle of the queue and went through the gauntlet. The Major took my papers, gave them a glance and handed them back. I was elated but with due decorum. The only other item of note that night was the most God awful meal given us. It was my second worst meal in the Army. The worst was at the transit camp at Stranraer in Scotland on the 13th February 1945 on my first day of Army Service. Very little of either meal was touched, if any.

By this time we were all thoroughly bored with flying. There was no magic left at all. Sitting in a bucket seat for an average of seven hours a time with the drone of those engines and no stewardesses was a world without romance. I had found that sleep came easier if I went to the rear of the plane and stretched out on the rows of kitbags stored in the baggage space. This idea soon caught on and I was often one of several doing the same thing. On then to Columbo of which I can remember nothing. The next stage was Changi barracks in Singapore, where we changed into our Khaki Drill. The Khaki Drill had been shoved in our kitbags, so you can imagine what a sight we looked. Still, we weren't allowed out, and nobody had any further aspirations for wine, women and song in any event. While at Singapore, we were paid four dollars in American script in preparation for the next stage which was the Philippines. I have no idea in which part of the Philippines we landed, and this was typical of the whole flight. The R.A.F. crew made no contact with the common herd of the Army whatsoever, and if any information was given to the Army officer on the plane, he kept it to himself.

I can only remember that the airfield was vast, and every conceivable establishment was there for the comfort of the Yanks − churches, cinema and anything else that was required to make it like "home sweet home". We soldiers were given instruction that we could only visit the P.X. canteen. For the life of me, I can't now remember if we were given a meal at this airfield, but I do vaguely remember that the Yanks had a strict rule about the dining hall. It shut at a certain time and, in no circumstances, would it be open again until the following morning. We had made the longest flight on this stage, something like eight and a half hours in the air, and so we arrived when the evening was well advanced. I know that four of us decided we had to visit the P.X. restaurant. Sitting at a table, we were greeted by Philippino maidens in charming fashion. On being handed the menu, I and the others felt a wave of embarrassment creeping up from the soles of our feet to the top of our heads. Great Britain was still on rations and our restaurant experience was nil. Fred's Cafe was the ultimate for a normal family eating out, and then the menu was limited to those items which did not require coupons. By 1950 it was, of course, possible to eat out daily without coupons, but we were still very out of practise. Coming from Germany especially, where war time conditions still prevailed, we squaddies were right out of our depth.

The main reason for our embarrassment was the price of the dishes. Chicken, under about twenty different titles, started at seven dollars. Steaks started at ten dollars. On the fourth page of the menu, we discovered something called 'Meatloaf' and priced at two dollars eighty. We ordered that on its own. The waitresses were vastly amused at our rejection of any suggestion of something called side orders, and neither did we order any drinks or dessert. On arrival, the Meatloaf was a vast amount of delicious eating. We would call it mince, but this meal was a real concoction of spices and herbs. Not only that but the large plate contained French Fries and a huge salad. We were well satisfied with our meal but we could not leave a tip. With hindsight, I imagine the extra's on the plate were given us out of pity, but maybe that sort of thing was normal in America. I still don't know.

Of one thing I am certain. Our embarrassment was the fault of a niggardly Government who wanted the most for the least when it came to dealing with common soldiers of whatever rank. Later on, in Korea, there were other red face occasions when we compared our lot with the Yanks – and all of them avoidable!

CHAPTER FOUR

Almost There

The last flight of our crusading journey was to Japan. Once again, we simply had no idea of what part of Japan we landed upon. Nobody saw fit to inform us. I suppose with scratching around I could now find out, but that would betray the general theme of this saga. This is my recollection of my experiences in the Korea War and I don't want to smooth out any bumps to appease my senior officers.

From the airfield we were taken to number 1098 Reinforcement and Transit Battalion, United States Army. I am not at all sure of the number or the title of this unit, but the Yanks seemed to take pride in using as many digits as possible in the unit title. I suppose it was a code rather than an indication of the number of Reinforcement Battalions. We were to spend about thirty six hours in that camp, and we were to have our eyes opened in more ways than one. I expect there was a PX at that airfield but we didn't dare make enquiries as to its whereabouts. I seem to remember getting rid of my remaining dollar at some outside kiosk selling chocolate.

Some of the lads found a quartermaster's store which would issue any equipment or clothing we would care to take away, providing we signed the register. By the time I got there, we appeared to have outstayed our welcome, but I did manage to sign for a walking out belt. In my present condition I could not use the belt and actually never did. What I really wanted but didn't dare try for was a poncho. This was a large square shaped piece of waterproof canvas with a hole in the centre for the head. This article could also be rigged as a makeshift tent and was far, far superior to the British Army groundsheet. The British shower protection was an odd shape for which I have no explanation. If you think of the human body lying flat, there was a larger part which accommodated the shoulders then tapered down to a more narrow part. One side was curved and had buttonholes down its length. In the centre of the curve was something like a collar which could be fastened round the neck when the groundsheet was worn as a cape. You could have it long in the front and short at the back, or vice versa, but even for small men the covering was at best no further than the crotch. In theory, two groundsheets could be buttoned together to form a tent, if you had stakes, rope and a ridgepole.

This article had been with us since before 1914 and, in typical civil service fashion, was never allowed to be improved upon.

Later, of course, the British bought thousands of ponchos from America before developing our own new type groundsheet which was an exact copy of the American weather protector.

Luckily for us, in Korea there was very little rain in the first month, and after that it was only snow which never thawed until about March, and then only during the day. At dusk it all froze up again. We may have suffered extremes of frost and we remained dry, but with no thanks to our utterly outmoded weather protection.

Anyway, word got around that we were shipping out of that camp to go by truck to a seaport to catch a ferry to Korea. Once again we took all our clothing and equipment with us. As we went through the dockyard gates, I noticed dozens of prostitutes waiting at the entrance to pick up sailors and others who were going ashore for the night. It was all rather blatant and emphasised the need of the average American serviceman to advertise his manhood. Whether or not the whore was used for payment, it seemed to be essential that the Yank was seen to be at least making enquiries about the price.

Before we finally part company with Japan, I must relate a story which emphasises the difference in attitude between the Americans and the British in regard to the fighting soldier. Although, by British Army standards, we had some luxurious meals in the Camp dining hall, we were in for a surprise and inadvertently caused ourselves some acute embarrassment and shame. When we had received notice to embark, we were also told that our last meal would be later than usual and after the camp staff had finished theirs. We duly attended for this meal, and even we could tell an extra effort had been made by the cooks. It was roast chicken with all the extras. Squaddy after squaddy loaded up the plates from the self service counter, and the cooks were beaming. However, despite our efforts there was still an enormous amount of food left. I wondered myself if there were other troops still to arrive. By the time we had finished, the cooks were no longer beaming and the Mess Sergeant was scowling. Mess Orderlies kept coming over and urged us to go back for more, which we did. Still there was a mountain of untouched chicken. We felt there was something wrong but did not know what. Mind you, we offered no thanks for the magnificent banquet, but then no common British soldier ever did that. Rather we cursed our cooks under our breath for stealing our rations.

Later the next day, we discovered that the Mess Sergeant had made all his Staff stay late for the privilege of cooking for the fighting troops. In addition, he had roasted one whole chicken for each and every British soldier. Sadly, we just did not have the stomach capacity for his generosity. Cordial relations between Allies took a hard knock that night.

In defence though, I must point out that although we had a Major, a Captain, three Lieutenants, a Company Sergeant Major and three Sergeants, contact between them and us was absolutely minimal. We were only paraded once, and that was to inform us when we would be leaving for the ferry. No information or advice was ever passed down and, throughout our tour in Korea, that was usually the normal situation. Keep the troops in the dark!

Although we were sailing overnight, there was no sleeping accommodation on the ferry. Just a large open space between decks with a covering of matting. We just slumped down where we were, but I must say there was ample space for us all. We were even given a demonstration, by an American soldier, showing us how to strip down, clean and reassemble an M.1. carbine. I should have taken more notice, as I later acquired a carbine from a dead Chinese but never tried to clean the weapon. Dawn saw us disembarking in Pusan in the far south of Korea, and we spent the first day and night in a warehouse. For those who have never tried to sleep on concrete, I strongly advise – don't attempt it now. It's sheer murder.

The next day finally saw us formed up into a proper rifle company. There was the Company Commander – a Major, the Second-in-Command – a Captain, three Subalterns commanding a platoon each, a Company Sergeant Major – (Warrant Officer Class Two), and three Sergeants as Second-in-Command to the Subalterns. I don't quite know when and how we acquired the Colour Sergeant – (Company Quartermaster Sergeant) – but he had not come over in our draft. Apparently, he was supplied by the Regiment – a Sergeant promoted for the purpose.

In those days, a Rifle Company Headquarters consisted of a Major, a Captain, a Company Sergeant Major, a Company Quartermaster Sergeant and storemen, a Company clerk, a Signalman and a couple of batmen/runners plus a Medical Orderly and two stretcher bearers, but I don't think we had those last three. The Platoon, of which there were three in the Company, had a Subaltern, a Sergeant, a batman/runner, a signalman, and a two inch mortar crew, a Lance Corporal and a Number One and Two on the mortar. All these odd bods came under the control of the Sergeant, leaving the subaltern to reign free and unfettered. There were three rifle sections in a Platoon. A Corporal in command of a section with a Lance Corporal in charge of the Light Machine Gun (The Bren) but who was also Second-in-Command of the Section. The Bren gun had a number one (the firer) and a number two who carried a lot of magazines and the spare parts wallet and spare barrel. There were six riflemen. Ten bodies in all.

And so, I found myself in command of number Four section of Eight Platoon of 'C' Company of the 1st Battalion of the Middlesex Regiment. It had been decided by the way that we would form 'C' Company in its entirety as this company was missing from the make-up of the Regiment when they landed in Korea. I was pleased that my platoon commander was that very soldierly looking person who I had noticed coming over on the plane. The Platoon Sergeant was an old veteran of thirty four years of age but who looked older with a handlebar moustache. He had seen service in the Desert and Italy during World War Two.

My Section were all strangers to me. We had not even travelled on the same plane together. I did not have a Lance Corporal and so one was chosen for me from among the Private Soldiers. This was a chap I will call Turnip. He appeared to be quite sensible with an air of authority. Turnip accepted the stripe and the one shilling and sixpence a day that went with it, but from there on made not the slightest attempt to carry out his duties as my second-in-command or as the NCO in charge of the Bren Group. He kept very much to himself and said little. If I had to leave the Section for some reason and instructed him to take over, he simply ignored me. The men in the section quickly learned that they had to supervise themselves and allocated the work load between them. They were very loyal in this respect. One other chap I shall mention at this time, and that was Shamrock. An Irishman of thirty eight years of age who had served with the Irish Guards throughout World War Two, which included the campaign of Norway, the Desert, Italy and Normandy. It was Shamrock's proud boast that he had never risen above Guardsman and had served time in Detention Barracks in every campaign. I found this boast hard to believe about Norway, as that campaign was so short, but I later learned it was time served in cells of a Royal Navy ship.

Shamrock, on discharge from the Army in 1946, had gained an appointment with the Corps of Commissioners. This organisation only employs ex-servicemen of the highest moral character and a clean conduct sheet. I rather think the Irish Guards used their influence in a last desperate attempt to let

Shamrock make something of himself. He let them down within twelve months by holding his hand out for tips in too blatant a fashion. When he rejoined the Army, (The Queen's Regiment), he must have been about thirty-four years of age and I rather think the Brigade of Guards used their influence once again. By his own admission, Shamrock was thoroughly immoral and unreliable, and he proved that self-assessment in Korea. Before Turnip had accepted the Lance Corporals' stripe, it had been offered to Shamrock, but he turned it down with emphasis.

"I've never worn a stripe in my life and I'm not going to start now!"

For me, the real tragedy of Shamrock was that he was allowed to volunteer for Korea at all. I presume someone in the Queen's Regiment took the opportunity to get rid of an undesirable. By the way, Shamrock was married with two teenage children.

Before I leave Shamrock, there was one other point about him I remember. He never ever mentioned being under fire from the Germans or Italians in any campaign. In the early days, I rather looked to Shamrock for guidance of what to do when we came under fire, but I received no help whatsoever.

Anyway, once we were formed into a company, we were issued with our weapons. A full rifle company required about one hundred and sixteen weapons on an individual basis, and these are, rifles, about ninety-two, Light Machine Guns (Bren), nine sub-machine guns (Sten), and revolvers, five or six. In addition, there were three two inch mortars – one for each platoon. Of these last, only the mortar would be carried on a day of need basis. The mortar bombs were very heavy and would be issued only for a set piece attack or in a defensive position. Truth to tell, I don't think we had any mortars at all. If we had any, I can't remember them being used.

For me and my section, there was first a Sten gun issued to me. It was an old Mark Two manufactured during World War Two and long since discarded in favour of the Mark Five of more recent manufacture but, in any event, it worked just fine when I had to use it. I had only three magazines of 9MM ammunition instead of the customary four but they sufficed. Lance Corporal Turnip and six riflemen and the person designated as Number Two on the Bren were issued with Number Four Lee Enfield rifles, all of ancient dates, and a bandolier of fifty rounds of .303 Ammo.

When these rifles were handed out, my years of experience as an instructor of weapons came back at me like a blow to the stomach. For at least fifty years and possibly more it was recognised that a rifle issued to a recruit became his very own personal weapon and his alone. The reason for this is very simple. No two persons look through the sights of a rifle and on to a target in the same way. Neither do two rifles behave in the same manner when a round of ammo explodes in the breach. The rifle is therefore "fitted" to the soldier by test firing on the rifle range. Each recruit fires a number of rounds at a target at just one hundred yards, and the result is analysed by the coach. The centre of the group must be at the centre of the target. If it isn't, adjustments are made to the size and position of the foresight and the recruit sent back to fire another group. When the recruit can get his group in the centre of the target, his rifle is "Zeroed" and the foresight fixed in position.

For all practical purposes, the issue of these rifles in such circumstances meant that any soldier firing at a target more than two hundred yards away would almost certainly miss. In any event, as I later discovered, I doubt if any of my lads could have hit the side of a barn at one hundred yards. The question of marksmanship in Korea was purely academic.

The issue of the Bren gun though was even more haphazard. Not knowing the past history of my section, I had to leave it to them to nominate a chap to be Number One on the L.M.G. This turned out to be a well-built three year regular with an utter contempt of all authority. Private Carrot had obviously been in trouble with the Police before joining the Army and his only ambition was to leave the service as quickly as possible. Neither did he care what trouble he caused during his enforced stay. Most young soldiers preferred the prestige of being the Number One on the Bren, but there was a snag. A rifle weighed seven pounds but the Bren weighed twenty three. The Number Two on the Bren was a thankless task for even the most dedicated soldier. Apart from carrying a rifle and fifty rounds of ammunition, he also carried a spare barrel for the Bren, a spare parts wallet and six magazines filled with twenty eight rounds. Each magazine weighed three pounds. As far as Korea went, it was all rather "pie in the sky" I'm afraid.

A fully equipped rifle section carried twenty three Bren magazines between them. Three by the Number One, six by the Number Two and two each by the Lance Corporal and six riflemen. However, Number Four Section was issued with only the Bren Gun and three magazines. There was no Spare Barrel or Spare Parts Wallet. It was months before we got a Spare Barrel and Wallet, and only two more magazines. Thankfully, we were never in a position where we ran out of loaded magazines.

CHAPTER FIVE

Still No Contact with the Enemy

Once we were formed up into a rifle company we moved out to somewhere near the front line, or at least that's what we were told. If it was the front line, there was a remarkable lack of precautions against a sudden attack by the enemy. Anyway, it was all designed to get us in the right frame of mind. We were set to digging slit trenches with our entrenching tools. These tools were a short wooden handle with a fitting to take a spade which fitted at right angles to the haft, so that the spade was used like a hoe. The other end of the handle had a fitting which enabled a bayonet to be slotted on – the idea being that in the middle of digging we had a weapon in case of a surprise attack. Nobody felt comfortable with this idea as the entrenching tool was considerably shorter than a rifle. In any case, when did soldiers ever dig a trench in view of the enemy without their rifles being very close to hand? Still, it was a well intentioned gimmick.

For myself, I never again used that entrenching tool for any purpose whatsoever. It simply hung from my belt at my back and was completely forgotten. Many were the times when I could have done without the extra weight, but it never occurred to me to throw it away. I was a fully automated robot of a soldier and obeyed the orders and regulations passed down to me from high.

In addition to other matters, our personal equipment and clothing was organised into three distinct types. The first was those items which we wore or carried at all times, i.e., cap, battledress, boots, anklets, shirt, vest, underpants, socks, groundsheet and all the fighting order of webbing equipment. Small pack, pouches, belt, braces, water bottle, bayonet frog and bayonet. In our small pack were mess tins, spare socks, housewife, spare laces, soap, towel, shaving kit, toothpaste and brush, pen and writing pad, field dressing, a comb and, in my case, a book to read. That particular book was a soft cover by Dorothy L. Sayers about Lord Peter Wimsey. It took me about three months to read that story, but was a life saver. Whenever there was a spare moment in the daylight, I would take it out for a read of just a few lines. The distractions were so varied and many that it was rare for me to read a whole page at one time, but I thank Dorothy for saving my sanity.

While I am writing, I remember we also had a tin mug and a knife, fork and spoon. My own personal collection of items included a mirror, a pair of scissors and a packet of plaster dressings. I am sure there were other items but, in the main, the common soldier in my Company carried absolutely nothing that would relieve the boredom. One or two more worldly wise carried a pack of cards, but their use was soon discarded in favour of keeping their hands warm with two pairs of gloves.

For the first couple of days, the amount of equipment we had to carry was bearable, but then came some additions. For instance, there were picks and shovels. In theory, these items would be issued when required, but we were engaged in an unknown war and so we each had a pick or shovel to carry. In spite of the extra weight, we never complained about these very useful tools. They were an absolute Godsend in the rocky, frozen country of Korea. There were also two hand grenades weighing a pound and a half each. On top of everything else, we started each day with a pack of 'C' rations supplied by the American forces. We ate the midday meal first followed by the evening meal and then the breakfast meal the next morning, by which time we were issued with another box to carry tied across the top of our packs.

Our second layer of equipment was the large pack. This was stuffed full with spare shirts, socks and underwear. In the early days it also contained a pullover. Within a short space of time the pullover was added permanently to our bodies. The large packs for the whole Company were carried on the three ton truck in the charge of the Colour Sergeant; the idea being that, at the end of the day, we would have access to our large packs in order to swap over any articles of clean clothes with the ones that required laundering. Fairly soon it was discovered that we rarely saw the truck at the end of any one day and, sometimes, not for a fortnight. As a consequence, we began to carry a spare shirt, spare woollen vest and underpants and a third pair of socks rolled up in the groundsheet and tied to the underside of the small pack.

More and more we were beginning to appear like pack mules and feel like them. We also learnt never to change any item of clothing unless we could wash and dry the soiled items in the same place where we were dug in. Sometimes we were caught out and had to carry the items wet. Yet another increase in the weight we were carrying.

The third layer of equipment was our kitbags. Into this crammed our overcoats, second pair of boots, plimsolls, third shirt, fourth socks, respirator and other items. Once the kitbag was packed, we never saw it again until the regiment returned to Hong Kong. My own kitbag was secured with a metal carrying handle and a padlock. Because of my precaution my kitbag was returned to me intact. Private Sprout, who I will mention again and again in this narrative, was left with one sock and his respirator.

However, I will unburden my soul about the hated respirator, or gas mask, as it was known to the civil population. Quite rightly, the gas mask during World War Two was issued to every serviceman or woman and every civilian. By law, the gas mask was carried everywhere and by everyone, including school children. By about the end of 1941 the civil population "forgot" about them, but servicemen continued to carry them for another year or so when on leave or on pass. By 1945, when I joined the Army, we were trained on a smaller version, but didn't wear the respirator on all training parades and never by itself at any time. Even so, I was very surprised when we were ordered to pack them away in our kitbags. The respirator was the sort of thing the authorities loved to insist should be carried at all times, "just in case". Evidently the message had got home at last even though the respirator was carried all the way from Europe to Korea. It was to be many more years before the respirator ceased to be issued as a personal item of equipment, but we have the threat of nuclear warfare to thank for that.

For the life of me, I can't remember when we were first issued with the American combat clothing, but it must have been fairly soon after arriving – and so, on top of the battledress we wore the American jacket and trousers and our berets were replaced with the combat cap. All three items were superb in quality and very efficient for their purpose. It took another ten years for the British to replace the woollen battledress with the more superior man made fibre of the combat gear, but tradition is very hard to break. For the moment though, we of the regiment were highly delighted.

I will now outline the clothing we wore for the next eight months. From the skin, there was a string vest, (never changed or washed but rather useless anyway), a woollen vest, a shirt, a pullover, (also never changed or washed), a battledress blouse, (likewise never exchanged for a clean item), and the U.S. Combat jacket. By this time, we were also wearing a camouflage net as a scarf. Lower down, we had woollen long johns, battledress trousers and combat trousers. Our feet only had one pair of socks and British Army boots. Woefully inadequate in the circumstances! On our hands were just the normal woollen gloves. If it wasn't for the ladies of the County of Middlesex sending us woollen mittens, we would have all suffered frostbite.

Over the next few months, we all suffered dreadfully with frozen hands and feet, especially the feet. In Britain, most people have made the complaint at some time, "I can't feel my feet! They're frozen right through!" Usually the circulation is soon restored in front of a fire. In Korea, when we had frozen feet, it also applied right up to the knee. Being in that condition for twenty four hours at a time was quite usual. Forty eight hours was not uncommon, and once I went for two weeks without "feeling my feet" even when asleep.

Although we were still in the area of Pusan at the far south of Korea, I had my first "casualty". One of my men had been a signaller in Germany and he was now taken from me and placed with the regimental signal platoon. This made it awkward for the rota of sentries during the night when two men were required to be on guard at all times. It was soon established though by custom that we all took turns at having a "night in". This brings me to another innovation I started, and one which made me very, very unpopular with the other NCOs.

A normal Quarter Guard in barracks would consist of a Guard Commander, a Deputy and six sentries. For night time purposes, each pair of sentries would have two hours on duty and four asleep. Taking the night to start at six in the evening and finishing at six in the morning, each set of sentries would be changed over twice. In reality, the sentry would have only four hours sleep a night, but the next Quarter Guard may be weeks away. In Korea, the hours of darkness lasted for thirteen hours and we put out sentries every night. We soon learned that the only warm place in Korea was our bed space, and it took an effort to get up just once during those thirteen hours.

Accordingly, I established a routine where the sentry rota was divided into just three shifts. If eight men took part, each man was in the slit trench for three hours and fifteen minutes. If six men took part, the tour of duty was four hours and twenty minutes – a very long time for any sentry, but it was preferable to getting woken up twice when the temperature was twenty five degrees below zero! Incidentally, in January the whole four hours and twenty minutes were spent marking time on the spot. If we stopped, we froze.

As to my unpopularity – after just two days I realised that the ordinary rifleman was destined to spend a huge amount of time standing in a slit trench during the hours of darkness. Naturally, he would resent the Corporals spending the whole night between blankets and would take any opportunity to shirk his duty. Therefore, I placed myself and my Lance Corporal on the duty roster. According to all military tradition,

I should never have started this system, but it was a terrific boost to morale among my men and, in turn, they all showed me a lot of loyalty in the days to come. My name was mud among the other section commanders, but they all had to conform or face mutiny. No Officer or Sergeant ever made a comment on this practise but, in any event, they spent every single night between their blankets for the whole thirteen hours.

There were other adaptions to the sentry system. For instance, if there were only nine or seven men in the section, then only eight or six men stood sentry. The odd man had a "night in" and, of course, we all took a turn at being the odd man. Every day a battalion order was issued as to the number of sentries that were to be on duty. It was either two per section or one per section. The section commanders would make an unspoken assessment of each daily situation and act accordingly. If it was rather tense at "the front" then two sentries it would be. If it was rather quiet, then one section only would supply two sentries throughout the night. The other two sections would have a lie in.

In my platoon at least this system was never abused. We all knew exactly where we stood on the rota for a night off, and there was never any bickering. If the reader thinks I have made rather a lot of sentry duty, you must remember the two most important items on a rifleman's agenda was first food and, secondly, sleep. Anything else was a long way off third, and that included fighting. I also point out that in eight months, not once did the Platoon Commander ever rise in the night to visit the sentries. It wasn't actually necessary with my men, but that is beside the point.

CHAPTER SIX

To Grips With The Enemy – At Last!

After only two days or so at playing soldiers, the whole battalion was trucked to an airfield where there were a number of "Flying Boxcars" standing by to fly us to the new battlefield. General Douglas McArthur had made a brilliant landing at Inchon, which was far to the North and quite near the 38th Parallel, the border between North and South Korea. The North Korean army far to the south had no option but to make a headlong retreat back up the way they came. We flew up to an airfield just south of Seoul, the capital of South Korea. In doing so, we flew over hundreds of thousands of North Koreans now stranded in the ridge of hills which formed a backbone in the Korean peninsular. Most of that army struggled back to the north, but even a year later there was still sporadic fighting going on in those hills.

The "Flying Boxcars" were so called because that is what they looked like – a huge railway wagon with wings. To the rear it was just like a hatchback car. A flap opened upwards and we filed inside. My Company had, of course, previous experience of flying, but for the rest of the regiment it was something new. We sat down in two rows facing each other with baggage between the rows. For some reason I felt a little uneasy as we actually sat on a parachute. The crew came along showing us how to strap on the chute. They were all very cheerful with jokes.

We took off with an enormous roar of engines, and that noise continued throughout the flight. In spite of everything, I dozed off, but was woken by a terrific clattering from the engines. "Oh, my God!" I said to myself. "We're going to crash." I checked the straps of the parachute and sat waiting for the order to bale out. I glanced at my companions but they were all looking to the rear. "Just like me," I thought, waiting for the order. Then there was utter silence and the hatch slowly moved upwards. There was a cloud base swirling around and then I was taken by surprise. Human figures were actually walking on the clouds. They started shouting something and came into the plane. It took at least another half minute for me to realize that we had already landed and were now unloading. I undid my straps and walked into the ground mist hoping none of my colleagues had spotted my confusion.

We spent the night in some abandoned huts on the airfield and were fed by the Americans from some field kitchen or other. The following morning we were taken by trucks through the recent battlefields. The Commanding Officer had let it be known that we were to take up positions facing the enemy. Part of the route was a road between paddy fields. On each side of the road slit trenches had been dug and for a quarter of a mile the road and the trenches were in a perfectly straight line. The trenches had been occupied by scores of North Koreans. Then came the American Sabre jets. The planes went down each side of the road, pouring out instant death. Bodies were everywhere. Some still in the trenches, some just outside, but none further than three yards away. There had also been a fire of some sort, and most of the bodies were scorched. I didn't want to, but I forced myself to look at everything. I reasoned that I had to get used to this sort of thing if I were to really become a leader.

One of the dead, at the moment of death, had his trousers down at his ankles and was now lying forward with legs dangling in the trench and upper body lying flat, face downwards. His exposed buttocks were burnt black. Some of the lads, after a joke that was then going around, shouted, "Well done, Percy. Bottoms up!" The ribaldry was only to hide their own fears, but it was better than breaking down. I happened to notice also that Lt. Plumb, sitting in the front seat of the truck, was staring straight ahead. Not by a glance, either left or right, did he indicate he could see the terrible sights of battle. Although I was glad he was my Platoon Commander, I now felt a little doubt creeping in. Even so and despite many indications to the contrary, I firmly believed that an officer was automatically courageous, and a fearless leader in battle. Right to the last, I stuck to my beliefs but, in the end, I was betrayed by my own conception of what a commissioned officer should be.

Later on during that frightening introduction to the battlefield, there was another rather intriguing sight. A bomb had been dropped by the American airforce and had made a vast crater between the road and a nearby village. Lying with her feet near the edge of the crater was a young Korean woman on her back. Not a hair on her head was disturbed, and her white clothing was still spotless. She looked so calm and peaceful but was dead nonetheless. Such is the peculiar effect of high explosive. Anyway, we finished our journey and bedded down for the night. The following day, we reversed the journey, saw all the corpses once again and finished back where we had started. With hindsight, I rather think the journey was arranged as a deliberate shock introduction to the battlefield. I myself never acquired a taste for examining dead bodies, although it was sometimes part of my job. Lt. Plumb, on the other hand, avoided all contact with the dead under any circumstances and was swiftly condemned by his own men for his timidity. After that first week he was never to be recognised as a leader.

Pushing on past Seoul, the capital of South Korea, we saw a great many fires raging and presumed it was the work of the retreating North Koreans. However, the Americans always had a policy of shooting first and asking questions later. Neither did the Yanks make any particular distinction between the civilians of North and South Korea. The battalion was set to follow the American Paratroops towards the border. I'm not sure even now if we actually crossed the 38th parallel, but I believed it at the time.

The Yanks had come under fire from a village about fifty yards from the road and, in return, had blasted the cottages with small arms fire and light artillery. However, they had not sent troops in to clear the village of the enemy, preferring to continue in a headlong advance north. The clearance was left to the Middlesex Regiment and my Company in particular. The ground between the road and the village was littered with the enemy dead and they had all fallen as though they had made a suicidal charge towards their enemy. There was no evidence that the Yanks had suffered any casualties.

My platoon was lined up to advance across the open ground towards the village. We had already seen corpses from a truck, but now we were walking around or over them. Halfway across, one of my men shouted, "I think this one is alive!" I looked at the body indicated and saw an enemy soldier in rather better clothing than the others. What worried me though was that both hands were tucked under the chest. We had already heard stories about fanatics who pretended to be dead but suddenly sprang to life, and holding grenades with the pins removed. The resulting explosions would kill the fanatic but also anyone else around. I told my rifleman to put a bullet into the body but, before he could comply, the enemy soldier sprang to his feet with arms raised and a broad smile across his face. For a Korean, he was a magnificent specimen. Tall and well built and looking more Caucasian than Mongul. He also carried a sub-machine gun and a pistol.

My Platoon Commander was going frantic in keeping us advancing in a line abreast. He chose to ignore the prisoner. I made signs to the Korean to give himself up to Company Headquarters, who were watching events from the road. He went off to surrender and I turned back to keep my section in line. I haven't the faintest idea what happened to the Korean after that; which brings me to a point of Army Training which has puzzled me for fifty years or more. Who takes care of an enemy soldier after he surrenders?

Neither in my recruit training nor the later advanced instructor training was this point ever mentioned. In the layout of an Infantry Battalion every member, from the Commanding Officer down to the ordinary rifleman has a specific task to perform. Nowhere in any manual of my day was the care of prisoners allocated to any one body of troops.

In the various large scale training exercises in Germany, one battalion would make a mock attack on another battalion, and umpires would decide which side won. Invariably some of the troops being attacked would put up their hands in mock surrender and the umpire would say, "You are prisoners!". The "prisoners" would then make their own way back to their regiment in order to fight another day. But what happens in a real war, I simply don't know. Obviously, if a Platoon makes an attack on an enemy position and prisoners are taken, then those prisoners must be dealt with. The Platoon Commander must then detail sufficient numbers of his own men to take the prisoners to the rear and, eventually, to a Prisoner of War Camp. But who takes over the prisoners from the attacking troops? I simply don't know. The situation is not dealt with in the Training Manuals.

The reader must also bear in mind that should an attacking force suffer any killed or wounded and then have to detail escorts for the prisoners, then the attacking force is considerably reduced in effective fighting potential. Possibly of no further use for another battle that day. Anyway, I took no other prisoners for the rest of my Korean campaign, and so I am still no wiser on that particular issue.

CHAPTER SEVEN

The Unacceptable Face Of War

To get back to the village towards which we were advancing...
We were all in a highly nervous condition but still without
having fired a shot in anger. Indeed, it was to be a couple more
weeks before any of us discharged our weapons and, even then,
just two of us fired for real.

We reached the narrow entrance to the village and prepared
to advance through and search the cottages. While I am writing
this, a thought just struck me. Although there were a lot of
bodies scattered around, I can't remember seeing any weapons.
Did the Yanks pick them all up or what? Or were the North
Koreans running towards the road to surrender? Rather a
puzzle I'm afraid.

The first suspicion of any enemy was a man of about forty
years of age who came out of one of the cottages. He was
dressed in white but wearing an American army shirt. Was he a
soldier who had acquired the shirt during the defeat of the
Yanks in the push southwards? More than likely, it was a present
from some North Korean soldier who had looted a storehouse.
Perhaps it was an acquisition from the Black Market when the
two countries were at peace. In any event it was rather foolish
of the man not to have got rid of the shirt when the shooting
started.

In those days, I was not a political animal but I knew what a war was and who was doing the fighting. From the age of twelve when World War Two started, I read the papers, listened to the wireless and conversed with my mates at school and at work. I knew exactly what was going on as regards the big picture of World War Two. In my ignorance, I imagined that every person on earth was just as informed as I was. In 1950 I was part of another war, but I did not realise at the time that the majority of Koreans, both North and South, did not know they were at war until they were caught up in the shooting. Neither did they know who constituted the enemy. These villages had no telephone system or newspapers and, in most cases, there was no road either. Communication was by visitors, if any, who walked from one place to another.

In the circumstances, it was not surprising that the Korean had kept his khaki shirt on. He was utterly unaware of the danger he was in. We sent him to the rear to be questioned and carried on with the search. It was now that I had my worst experience of warfare. Worse even than being shot at and mortared. In going through the village, we discovered that all the cottages were shut up tight with not a sound from the inhabitants. No attempt was made to force the doors as we correctly assumed the enemy were either dead outside the village, or had fled. One cottage though had the door open and I could hear a sort of moaning. There was also a shell hole in the straw roof. I went inside and in the gloom I could see that everything was covered in a grey dust. I made out the form of a man, a woman and two children, all lying face down on the floor and very still. There was a third child lying on her back, and it was she who was making the noise. The same word was repeated over and over again and I presume it was the Korean word for "Mama".

Amongst all the grey was a splash of red. The child had a shrapnel wound stretching from her forehead to the back of her skull. Her eyes were open but there was just that one word being repeated. I slung my Sten gun over my shoulder, and bent down to pick up that innocent victim. I carried her outside and the tears were running down my cheeks. I had no idea as to what to do next, but an old woman came out of another cottage.

She had been waiting until it was safe to emerge and help the family in such distress. I handed over the child and after I was gone she went for help from our medical team. They did what they could, but I heard the next day that the infant had died. That was one memory of war that I have never forgotten. If anything, I became a more hardened soldier from that time on but, while I had no compunction about shooting an enemy soldier who was shooting at me, I never once considered taking up arms against helpless civilians. I don't know the circumstances that brought death to that family, and probably it was unavoidable but it had an effect on me that has remained with me for all of my life.

I know from experience that fear is the paramount emotion for any soldier in any battle. It is fear that forces a soldier to keep pumping bullets into a fallen enemy on the off chance that a fanatic may rise up and continue the fight – but where is the fear from a child or a woman or a very old man.

Even so, I have known whole villages of non-combatants wiped out by large forces of troops, but surely not all of those troops were afraid, and what were the officers doing? I can't explain the reason behind these massacres, but they happened.

In some cases the troops involved came from Near Eastern countries where this sort of conduct is normal practise and continues to the present day.

Neither I nor any of my comrades in 'C' Company had actually discharged our weapons in this incident, but had been prepared to do so if the necessity arose; but we had actually engaged in an act of war even if it was only to take one prisoner. Little did we know that it would take another two weeks and four hundred miles of travel before we came under fire. In between times there were enough incidents to last us a lifetime of story telling.

From that village, we followed the Yanks on a fast advance northwards, until we fetched up twenty miles from the Yalu river, the border between North Korea and Mongolia. We rarely travelled on foot but mostly on trucks or the backs of tanks. By now our Brigade consisted of the Middlesex Regiment, the Argyle and Sutherland Highlanders, the Third Royal Australian Regiment, a Regiment of New Zealand Field Artillery, an Indian Army Field Ambulance unit and a Troop from the Royal Corps of Signals. At first, we had no back up force such as the Royal Army Service Corps, Royal Army Ordnance Corps and Royal Electrical and Mechanical Engineers. For those type of support troops, we had to rely on the Yanks and this put the back up of our battalion Quartermaster. He in turn saw to it that troops at the front had exactly what was due in accordance with regulations and not one jot more. There were times when supplies of food could not get through and we went hungry. Even so, we still had the exact rations on the good days. Never was any attempt made to issue double rations to make up for our starvation periods.

On the way north our days became rather routine. We followed the Yanks in their pursuit of the enemy. It was a case of just sitting in trucks until a stop was made. We debussed and, if there was a hill in the vicinity, we climbed it and dug in. Digging a slit trench was priority in accordance with our tactical learning, but it soon became third in the essential order of things. Korea being a very rocky country, it was only on rare occasions that we actually dug down deep enough for a soldier to stand in for sentry duty and suchlike. At the best, the sentry was covered up to his waist, but usually only to his knees. What we did discover was that the first priority became the search for somewhere flat to lay out our bedding roll. We all had the experience of trying to sleep on a slope only to find we slid feet first down the hill. Likewise, a rough or rocky piece of ground prevented sleep. Therefore, when the Platoon Commander allocated the site of our intended slit trenches, we first sized up the ground for our sleeping places.

Often we had to clear a flat space with the help of our pick-axes and shovels. Before that task, however, I looked around the available space and made a decision as to the location of a latrine area. This was the very first priority. Having been the victim of misplaced night soil, I always made it plain to the section where we should drop our trousers or stand to urinate. I must say that my section always appreciated where we stood in this particular matter. Needless to say, no direction whatsoever came from the Platoon Commander about such matters, in spite of the importance of the planning required. Another little touch I taught my lads, and eventually the Company, was the adjustment of the ground to accommodate the human hip bone. Years before Korea, I had read of slaves or prisoners being transported across the Sahara. When a stop was made for the night, each slave would scrape a hole in the ground for his hip when lying on his side. Proper sleep on a hard flat surface is virtually impossible, as I had already discovered in my training days. Already in Germany I had been accustomed to digging a groove across the sleeping place in about the position the hips would take up. In the early days in Korea, I had been laughed at for this practise, but my fellow soldiers soon followed suit if they wanted some comfort.

Quite soon after arriving in Korea we established our priorities. Except when we actually came under fire, the War took a very low place in our attention span. Number One in order of importance was the matter of sleep and that in warmth, if possible. As time went on we were issued with a summer sleeping bag in addition to the blanket we carried. Then we were given a two man pup tent. This tent split into two halves for carrying, but I'm afraid I let my companion carry both halves. I was five feet four and rather puny, and he was a strong six foot two! I was very grateful for this concession but, in any event, I did a lot more running around as the Section Leader, so it was fairly even in regard to effort.

Also in the early days, a comfortable sleep depended on what clothing we kept on during the night. Very soon we wore it all, but our boots presented a certain difficulty. Keeping them on was warmer, but we were constantly kicking each other's ankles and shins. Leaving the boots outside meant that they froze and, in turn, meant an awful job getting them on in the morning. After trial and error, it was the general conclusion that it was better to leave the boots outside. When we had the benefit of the pup tents, the boots were kept inside the tent along with weapons, food and equipment. We regarded those days as sheer heaven marred only by the necessity of getting up at least once during the night for sentry duty and suchlike.

Number Two in importance was the matter of food. To be fair, it was only rare that we were short of food and, although we felt very deprived at times, we did not actually suffer in the physical sense. Probably did us good in the end! Even so, a lot of our waking hours were spent in preparing and eating our rations.

Number Three in importance was the gathering of fuel with which to thaw out our rations and to give us some degree of comfort during the day. The section camp fire was kept going all the time when in one position. When we were issued with the American 'C' rations the box contained, apart from other items, three tins of food which were already frozen. These tins had to be punctured twice at the top and then very slowly thawed out and heated before the food could be consumed. For that we had to have wood. When I talk about selecting a sleeping and latrine location at the top of a hill, what actually happened first was this.

We laid down our weapons, took off our equipment and then two men immediately went looking for wood for the fire. Without the fire we didn't eat and probably did little else. The camp fire was very, very important. The fuel may be a few twigs if we were in wooded terrain, but usually the wood came from the framework of a Korean house, if unoccupied.

In January 1951, for instance, we were in position alongside a deserted village. By the end of January, there wasn't a house remaining; just heaps of rubble and mortar. It wasn't a matter of wanton damage, but of sheer survival. When the temperature was down to twenty five degrees below zero we simply had to have a fire to crouch round.

I haven't mentioned water, as yet, but of course that was of paramount importance. There were numerous streams to quench our thirst until they froze over. Our water bottles froze solid in November and did not thaw out until February. In the meantime, we gathered snow to melt down in the section billycan. Four pints of snow makes one pint of water and alongside the search for wood went the gathering of snow. Luckily for us the snow never thawed out during late November and until late February.

Many different elements made up our day, such as letters from home, but basically it was sleep, food, fuel and water. The War affected us only as an after-thought.

CHAPTER EIGHT

North to the Yalu River

Actually, we never reached the Yalu but fetched up twenty miles short. However, we travelled a great distance in a very short time. At one time we advanced North fourteen times in fourteen days. Mostly we were in American trucks and once or twice on the back of tanks. Our travels on foot were only to go up a hill, dig in for the night, and come down to the road again in the morning.

After leaving the wounded child village, we passed another village which looked exactly the same. It stood off the road by about four hundred yards, and was apparently occupied by enemy troops as well as the civilian inhabitants. I wondered why no attempt had been made to engage the North Korean forces. Actually, I never asked anyone the question in my mind as it wasn't done for a mere corporal to doubt the tactics of his superiors. The Americans, and my own Commanding Officer, were well aware of the presence of enemy troops, and so I presumed they had other measures in mind. I can only surmise that the senior officers did not want another shambles as that which had just occurred. With hindsight, I now agree with that decision, but it did leave scores of North Korean soldiers the liberty to fade away into the hills. In any event, they were probably only looking for a chance to surrender. I myself suffered a feeling of outrage at the time. All my training had injected one simple principle into my very being. "When you see the enemy, you attack!" But we did not attack and I was left very confused.

In the following paragraphs I will describe a series of incidents that occurred on the advance North, but without relating any to a period of time. First though I will describe our own food situation. We were perpetually starving or thought we were. I only know we felt hungry all the time. Only one or perhaps two meals were given us each day and it was just not enough. The Yanks on the other hand were gloriously overfed. We were so envious but, being British, we thought that we were the better soldiers. I found out later that British stuck up pride prevented the senior officers from asking for assistance from the Yanks. In turn, our politicians expressly forbade any of the Quartermaster staff from feeding the troops from any source but our own. It was a matter of money, after all! Rations were rations, and the cost must never be exceeded no matter what.

Later on, common sense prevailed, and we were issued with American 'C' Rations and Oh Boy! What a joy they were! Three meals a day and extras like Chocolate, Crackers, Cigarettes and Toilet Paper. There was also Coffee and Cocoa in powdered form.

Although we were issued with these American 'C' Rations fairly soon after our arrival in Korea, we did not live with this luxury for very long. The average British soldier, being what he is, needs something to moan about. As always, food was the first complaint. A group of Londoners began griping about the Yanks' food and demanded a return to some decent British grub. I was against the whole idea, but I was a voice in the wilderness. We returned to the food being cooked by the

Colour Sergeant as and when he was able. There were never three meals a day; usually two, and sometimes only one. Matters improved only slightly when we went onto British composite rations, scale 'B' unbalanced. This was a box to be shared between five men. There was much bickering as to which five men should share the same box.

Invariably, I had to borrow two men from another rifle section to muck in with three of mine so that we could share two boxes. One day though the Platoon had a problem. Including the Platoon Commander and the Sergeant, there were only twenty four of us. The Colour Sergeant, an officious incompetent, refused to issue five boxes of rations to twenty four men. At the time a battle was raging only a short distance away, and we had been on the march and were exhausted. One ration in these circumstances was a very small item in a huge complex of conditions and events. Nonetheless the Colour Sergeant was adamant. We borrowed a chap from another Platoon who had a strength of twenty six and got our five boxes. While all this argy-bargy was going on, the Officers and Sergeants just looked away. Any one of them could have put the Colour Sergeant in his place, but they did nothing. I have always wondered why.

The poor chap we had borrowed for meals had to run over from his own trench when we called, get his share of food in his mess tins and run back to his trench, by which time his food was cold. The morale of the whole company was very low because of this arrangement. The 'B' rations weren't too bad on the whole, but were intended for troops in a static position. We, on the other hand, were constantly on the move. Quite soon, we simply had to go back to American one day, one man 'C' rations. There was never another complaint about food for the rest of our tour.

Before I leave the question of food, I must explain that our situation was further aggravated by the American attitude towards their fighting soldiers. Although every modern Army has to have far more troops at the rear than actual combat soldiers, i.e., Stores, Transport, Medical and suchlike, there was no question of equal rights in the Yanks' Army. If, for instance, food was in short supply, then the fighting soldiers came first. Every effort was made to ensure the front line soldiers had a full quota of rations. The troops that went short were those in the backwater bases. I doubt if any American soldier in the rear actually went short of food, but the principle was thoroughly understood and approved. In real terms, there was a great waste of food by the front line troops as, quite often, there were stockpiles of rations that could not be absorbed. In any event, every visiting Senator from Washington made it a priority to ensure that the rations were adequate and delivered on time. I will show later that the same attention was paid in regard to clothing and equipment.

The first part of our swift advance North brought us all the way to the outskirts of Pyongyang, the capital of North Korea, without any incident of note. Just the routine of standing to in our temporary hill top position, getting breakfast, and then moving on before going up another hill for the night. Like Seoul, we never actually went through the city but detoured around it. We could see huge fires burning as they were in Seoul when we went past that city, but any thought of looting was impossible for us. We were always stuck in a convoy. Once we did find a huge stack of abandoned North Korean bank notes. Prior to the war they must have had an exchange value of millions of dollars. We all snatched bundles of notes for ourselves, but gradually realised the notes were now just paper and, as paper, they were used for the obvious purposes!

Before leaving the area of Pyongyang, we had to cross over a very large bridge. Hundreds of Yanks were walking the length of the bridge, and we had to pause underneath it. Sitting with his back to one of the supports was a North Korean male of about twenty five years of age. He was clad in the usual white clothing of the working class. His face was a pulp of raw flesh; he had been battered by rifle butts. The Yanks, in explanation, said he was a spy. Just then, scores of American soldiers opened fire from the left railing of the bridge. Their target was a man, a woman and a child running through the rushes growing on the far bank of the stream. All were wearing the usual white clothing of the peasant class, but the man was wearing the particular black straw hat of a village elder. The man was seen to fall and a posse left the bridge to finish the business. One American, with bright shining eyes, made a particular point of telling us Limeys of the incident. "His eyes were still popping when we got there, but they are not popping now!" The Yank was almost delirious with excitement, but it never seemed to occur to him that the targets included a woman and a child as well as the old man. By no means whatsoever could any one of them be mistaken for soldiers.

In another incident, we had stopped for the night and as usual we went up a nearby hill to bed down. It was dark and some of our lads stumbled over two bodies. As usual, they came running to me to report their find. Although we had been together for only three weeks, and I was only one of three section commanders in the Platoon, it was always me who received these reports – never the Platoon Commander or the

Platoon Sergeant. By instinct, the lads knew I would do something. I went to look at the bodies and saw there was a man of about forty years of age and another of about twenty. The two of them were in civilian clothes and tied together with wire from a fence. Both had been shot in the back and in falling the younger had sprawled across the elder. From our position on the hill we could see right down on a village and I presumed the men came from there. No other Allied soldiers had been through the village and so the shooting could only have been done by the retreating North Koreans. Why! We never found out. I reported the incident to Lt. Plumb but he didn't want to know – as usual. Two weeks later, he came to me in a tearing hurry and wanted all the details. Word had got around, and the Intelligence Officer of the Battalion was very cross that the incident was never reported.

Then I lost my steel helmet. It was like this. We never wore our helmets but just used the chin strap to hook the battle bowler on to our small pack. Incidentally, the helmets were quite heavy. Anyway, when stopped to heat up our rations, the helmet was taken off the pack in order to get at our mess tins. My helmet in particular was very well camouflaged and almost invisible when placed upon the earth and grass. One day, in a hurry, I forgot to replace the helmet on the pack. At the next stop I discovered the loss. I was horror struck. I had never known anyone to loose a helmet and didn't know the cost. For any soldier to lose any equipment was a crime of gigantic proportions. Each member of the Armed Forces had a regulation set of equipment to lug around all over the world, and any loss was an automatic charge. There was no question of simply paying for a replacement. The offender had to be placed on a charge.

Even though the punishment was usually confined to paying for a replacement, there was still the matter of an entry on the crime sheet. For two weeks, I was a very worried NCO I kept hoping we would get shot at, very slightly, so that I could say I had lost the helmet in the excitement, perhaps when running down a hill – **anything!**

Then I was saved by a miracle. We were on top of a large ridge, getting ready for another days march. I hadn't told a soul about my enormous military offence but then the Company Commander sent round word that we could throw away our helmets if we so desired. There was a rousing cheer from the troops and a hundred or so helmets went flying down the hillside and, in pretence, so did mine. I was so, so happy! A few of the lads retained hold of their helmets but, in due course, and after a few more hills to climb, these were discarded as well.

CHAPTER NINE

More Incidents

Before getting down to our first real taste of combat, I must describe the crossing of a river by boats. Any river crossing, even at night, is very hazardous and must result in casualties if the enemy are aware of what is happening. The real snag is that there is absolutely no cover from the enemy fire. On land there are trees, bushes, banks of earth, crops and even grass that can absorb some of the missiles. On water there is no impediment whatsoever to the flight of a bullet.

One evening we were told that our company had been selected to lead the battalion in a crossing of a river. The river was very wide and we were to go across in assault boats using paddles as a means of propulsion. A very heavy artillery barrage would commence before dawn and last until the crossing was complete. The boats were stacked ready about two miles from the river. The launch was planned for 7am and 'A' Company were to carry the assault craft to the rivers edge. 'C' Company would then push out the boats, clamber in and start paddling. Fully loaded, as usual, we had quite a long march to arrive at the spot where the boats were waiting, and we were surprised to find the boats still there, but no sign of the carriers, 'A' Company. It was now about 6.30am.

Then the order came round. We, the assault Company, would have to carry the boats ourselves. The boats were made of metal and were very heavy. Eight men, four either side, lifted the boats on to their shoulders and we set off; through scrub, over ditches and across paddy fields. The haul took two hours of arduous toil and we arrived at the river bank. It was now 9am and the artillery barrage had ceased at 7.15am. There had also been a smoke screen but that was long gone. We were also surprised to find a party of American assault engineers awaiting our arrival. Apparently, two Yanks were to go across in each boat for the purpose of steering and returning the boat back to the other shore.

In typical British Army fashion, we clambered into the boats fully laden. Nobody thought to tell us to take off our equipment, making it easier to paddle and making it safer if we turned turtle.

The crossing for 'C' Company turned out to be fairly easy. We were near an estuary and the river was subject to tidal flow from the sea. Later parties had an awful time with grounding on mud banks and waiting to float off again. After a very long haul at the paddles we ground ashore in enemy territory. I rather think I was the first man ashore. I jumped out calling for my men to follow. I selected a ridge about fifty yards inward and got the section down into a firing position. We were at the side of a road leading towards a village. There wasn't a sign of life from either soldier or civilian. I heard the sound of motor vehicles and then I saw the vehicles. They were American trucks coming from my right and going north through the village. They had crossed the river by bridge half a mile upstream.

The whole river crossing was a complete sham – just an exercise to see how it would go for real. Not that the persons in charge would admit such a thing, not even forty years later. The lesson learned was that it was a complete shambles and just a dozen or so of the enemy could have wiped us out.

While I was in the act of drafting this paragraph, I read in the "Morning Calm", the newsletter of the Korean Veterans' Association, a letter from my former Platoon Commander. In this letter, he refers to the wounding of two members of the Platoon on the 27th October 1950. It was on this day that the Company first took part in a shooting war, and I feel that I can remember the details very well indeed. I can't remember any of our Platoon being wounded at all on that day, nor indeed any of our Company. It's just possible that I was out of sight of some of the Platoon for part of the time that day, but that no news of the wounding came my way is very strange – to me at least!

I will take up the story from the 26th October 1950. On that day, we were advancing through some hilly country and my Platoon were riding on the outside of American tanks. I was actually on the lead tank. Suddenly the tank stopped and then reversed in a hurry. On going round a bend in the road, with a steep hill on the left and a ravine on the right, we came upon a Russian T34 tank of the North Korean Army. Its main gun was trained on the bend in the road and couldn't possibly have missed such a sitting duck as the Yankee tank. It was only about forty yards away and, in armoured warfare terms, that was virtually muzzle to muzzle!

We, the passengers, were ordered off and told to take cover. There wasn't any cover but that was a mere detail in the circumstances. In a surprisingly short time, a decision was made by the Americans. It was supposed that the T34 had broken down and had been placed in such a position that would hold up our advance. It was also supposed that the T34 had been left fully manned in order to open fire on the lead American tank. As there was no fire from the T34 it was then supposed the crew had used their discretion and silently stole away. That discretion was extremely fortunate for the Yanks and their passengers. We would not have stood a chance in Hell.

Anyway, the Yanks decided to deal with the T34 once and for all. The lead tank drew back as far as it could and then pumped solid shot after solid shot into the T34. There may have been some high explosive as well, but we passengers had withdrawn well out of the danger zone.

Eventually we were ordered back onto our tank and the advance continued. We passengers could not tell the effect of the Yankee broadsides, but as the road wound around some hills and alongside the opposite side of the ravine, we later saw the T34 was beginning to brew up. Twenty-four hours later that Russian tank was still burning. My Company and probably the rest of the battalion got past the T34 before it started to go pop but, thereafter, the rest of the advancing troops had to run the gauntlet of exploding ammunition as well as the very fierce flames.

That night, we started to dig in as usual and for the very first time came under enemy fire. It was mortar bombs that came down at the rate of one every half hour or so. I saw the explosions of a couple and so it was still daylight. The last mortar bomb came down about 9pm. No casualties were reported from anywhere in the battalion, but I was an unreported casualty.

It happened like this. We had been allocated a position some way off the line of advance and as usual we were digging in. We had got down about eighteen inches when the call came round for one man to collect two men's evening meal from the mobile kitchen on the road. I sent my partner, Private Sprout, to collect our share. I was busy hacking away at the soil and rocks and, in the moonlight, I saw Sprout returning with a mess tin in each hand. Just then another mortar bomb was whining in our direction. The next thing I knew, I was flat on my back with the wind knocked out of me. I thought, "So this is what it's like being blown up!" I felt my limbs and body but could not find any breakages or wounds. However, I did have a recollection of two mess tins being thrown sky high and Sprout charging towards me. In his anxiety to find cover, Sprout had shouldered me out of the slit trench and had cowered down in the meagre hole we had dug. His backside though was well clear of cover. I picked myself up, persuaded Sprout to stand up, find the mess tins and go back for another meal.

Shortly after we stopped digging and settled down for the night. We had only to supply one sentry per section and I went on the first shift. I found a very convenient grassy bank and I sat down with the bank at my back. In what seemed like two minutes, I heard a scrabbling noise and voices. Not ten yards away was Lt. Raspberry of 7 Platoon together with several of his men. He had just returned from a patrol. He gave me a long hard look but said nothing. I stammered out the password and he replied and then led on back to his position. I looked at my watch and saw I had been sitting there for two hours fast asleep. I had visions of being shot at dawn, but heard nothing more.

CHAPTER TEN

Under Small Arms Fire

After the incident of the Mortar bombs, which was my Company's first time under fire of any sort, we then experienced small arms fire. It happened the following day. As opposed to shelling and mortars, which can land anywhere, rifle fire is much more personal. It is being purposely aimed at a body of men and the effect on morale is drastic. Despite the statistics which show that only one soldier is killed by rifle fire against ninety nine by other means, i.e. bombs, shells, mortars and mines, it only takes one rifle to generate the same fear as that raised by a battery of artillery. This theory is for myself alone, by the way. I have known too many soldiers who are frightened all the time, and that due to ignorance. With my superior training, I was able to assess, with some accuracy, the very real moments of danger. Not that I relished being under fire of any sort, but I was able to contain my feelings a little better than most.

This superior training did not stop me being shell shocked after eight months in Korea. I was just as bad a case of jangled nerves as the rest of the battalion. In typical "stiff upper lip" fashion, it is only now that I can admit to have been bomb happy for quite a long time after Korea – years in fact, but that is all another story!

Anyway, on this particular day 'A' Company had led the way on foot in the company of just one Yankee tank. The enemy had opened fire with high explosive from just one North Korean tank and three soldiers had been killed. 'A' Company stopped where they were and the advance was taken up by 'C' Company. As we marched forward, we passed the Padre carrying out the burial service for the three dead. Their grave was a ditch at the side of a paddy field. Many dead we had already seen, but this was different. They were ours!

The American tank crew had positioned themselves beside a Korean farmhouse and were exchanging shots with the enemy tank. One of the crew was pooping off burst after burst with the ×50 calibre machine gun. This gun is on the outside of the tank which leaves the gunner much exposed. Despite the high explosive and solid shot coming from the enemy tank, the Yankee gunner remained where he was. We heard later the gunner had been awarded the Silver Star – and well deserved!

'C' Company were ordered to take position on a small ridge to the right of the farmhouse. As the enemy were about eight hundred yards away, we infantry were only spectators at the moment. Shot after shot was exchanged between the two tanks but, in addition, American Sabre jets plastered the enemy position. We, the audience, watched the gun flashes from the North Korean tank and ducked our heads at the same moment as the incoming explosion. The velocity of those tank missiles was such that I doubt if we humans could have taken evasive action in time anyway. We still ducked though in automatic fashion.

From our upper circle, we infantry watched shot after shot go over, below, behind and in front of the enemy Armoured Fighting Vehicle and then one shot hit the tracks. The

Armoured Fighting Vehicle was on the move at the time but now it was stopped. We saw a hatch open and could just make out a figure clamber down, inspect the tracks and clamber back. Then the enemy tank moved off and vanished round a small hill. Too late, the Yanks fired several more shots, but they all landed behind the North Korean tank. Chivalry notwithstanding, the Yanks should have fired again while the Armoured Fighting Vehicle was stationary. The distance between the tanks was about eight hundred yards, the ideal range for tank warfare, but the moment of glory was lost. **Why oh why** did the American Tank Commander cease firing?

Following that incident 'C' Company were withdrawn from the ridge and ordered to continue the advance up the road towards the enemy position. For me though there was a slight pause. Beside the Korean farmhouse there was a thatched pen containing three young pigs. In typical Korean fashion, there was no gate to this pen. Once in, the pigs stayed there without room to roam around. Somebody though had set fire to the thatch. The pigs were being roasted alive. I put the barrel of my Sten gun between the bars and fired until there was no more movement. We in 'C' Company had not been in action long enough to undergo that callous indifference to suffering, which most fighting men develop, but I don't think either that the thatch caught fire accidentally.

In full view of the enemy, we formed up in normal marching order of three platoons and set off towards the hill. After about five hundred yards, we stopped, and then in very unhurried fashion spread across a very open field in three ranks. We were going to advance towards the enemy position without any covering fire. By chance, I was in the third rank when the order came to go forward. By the time we had gone one hundred yards there were no more orderly ranks, and I found myself in the front although I had not changed my pace. There were one or two shots that went overhead, but I don't think anyone really noticed. The Yanks later described our action as a text book deployment, but it was pure Victorian military desperation. As luck would have it our Commanders got away with it.

Arriving at the base of the hill, there was a hurried rearrangement of the ranks and the order was given to "Charge." We scrambled up the slope and arrived on a plateau. We could find nothing of the enemy and as usual were given the order to dig in. Before we could comply, however, my Platoon was ordered to go through an area of scrub that blocked the way to another hill further away. We lined up alright and started off. Because the scrub was thicker in some places than others the line quickly became staggered. One section with the Platoon Sergeant was ten yards in front of my section. The Platoon Commander was in line with me but thirty yards away. The other section was ten yards to my rear but much further away.

Suddenly, one of my chaps shouted, "There's a Gook in there!" and indicated a stand of canes. I looked and a Mongolian face turned towards me. In a split second, I also noticed the Platoon Commander was directly in line and behind the enemy. I swung up my Sten gun and fired a burst of two rounds. I knew I did not dare miss. The North Korean fell out of his cover and flopped about a bit. I ordered one of my men to fire at the still moving body, which he did. The enemy soldier was now still. The platoon carried on with the scrub clearance but, as soon as I could, I hurried back to my "trophy". I saw that I had put one bullet straight into the heart and the other in the centre of the chest. At least my years of training had paid off and the Platoon Commander had survived.

A search of the body revealed a document very similar to my own Pay book Parts One and Two. There was also a photo of a Korean woman but whether wife or mother I could not tell. I also saw that the Korean had another wound in his right kidney and at first surmised that came from my rifleman. I was wrong about that. The Platoon Sergeant pointed out it was a jagged wound from shrapnel and the soldier was already dead when I fired. He was most certainly wrong about that, but it gradually sank in that the enemy soldier was no threat to us whatsoever, and was probably trying to surrender. A search of his little "cave" showed his rifle standing up with the safety catch applied. The soldier had been in a kneeling position when he moved and at his knees was a now cold fire on which he had been cooking some raw meat. The shrapnel wound had been inflicted some two or three hours before; probably from the bombs from the air. There wasn't a trace of any other North Koreans nearby and nothing to explain what this soldier was doing all on his own.

My initial satisfaction at having made a kill was very subdued by the knowledge that the Korean need not have died, and I have been somewhat haunted by the incident ever since. Still, as they say, it **is** war!

Anyway, we finished clearing the scrub and went back to our original position. Digging in commenced, as usual. For a change the earth was quite pliable, and we were able to finish a set of decent slit trenches. We even had time for a rest before darkness set in. The whole Company were rather elated at this time. We had actually been under fire and had survived! Secretly, we all thought that warfare wasn't so bad after all.

I think this an appropriate time to mention the different degrees of fear to which soldiers are liable in Battle. All, and I mean all, are frightened to some extent, but the average combat soldier is able to continue with his duties when so ordered. Commanders of any rank are able to contain their fear by the simple expedient of giving orders. This necessity of command is a tremendous help in overcoming the desire to drop to the ground and stay there, no matter what! I myself found the requirement to give orders under fire a very steadying influence. The opportunity to show a better face to my fellow soldiers gave me more confidence. The poor rifleman though had no one to order about and, consequently, suffered more from actual fear and, in a lot of cases, imaginary fear stemming from ignorance of the actual conditions.

Some few unfortunate individuals never were able to contain their fear and were broken men for a time. Of course, we were all near that dangerous edge but just managed to carry on. It is interesting to note that when the battalion arrived back in Hong Kong, the Medical authorities were of the opinion that the whole battalion was bomb happy. How right they were!

However, despite the horrors of trench warfare in World War One, which drove millions to insanity, and the further experience of World War Two, there was a peculiar feeling in my battalion. It was all undercover and never mentioned out loud, but Battle Fatigue simply did not exist. No matter the conditions, nobody was allowed to give in to their fears. Of course, there **were** cases of officers and men being carried out of battle and without a visible wound. The excuse of the authorities was that if they gave in to one case, then everybody would be playing up. This in spite of the overwhelming esprit de corps which made Regular Soldiers and National

Servicemen alike keep on going rather than admit to fear to their comrades.

While I am rather down on my superior officers in regard to their attitude about shell shock, I must remember that those same officers were under the scrutiny of the British Government. Orders had been given to play down and avoid casualties. Reporting cases of Battle Fatigue was simply out of the question. It was all Baden Powell at the siege of Mafekin and the stiff upper lip in front of the natives.

More Incidents of War

After the incident of the unnecessary killing, I learnt that another shooting had taken place further along the line as we charged up the hill. An officer of the North Korean Army had come forward with his hands up in surrender. He was promptly shot dead by one of our Lance Corporals. Thereafter, that Lance Corporal was known as no end of a good fellow. Strange that!

While resting after the bush clearance, a couple of our chaps had discovered two pairs of boot clad feet sticking out of the ground. Two of the enemy had been buried in a very shallow grave but, such had been the hurry, the feet had remained exposed. We all thought that this was hilarious and a move was made to dig up the corpses for a closer look. The Platoon Sergeant, Sgt. Swede, put a stop to this, but the incident showed the way we were developing. We laughed at anything and everything. It was the beginning of shell shock but also a way of relieving the tension building up. Those who laughed were the survivors. Those that didn't laugh were the worst of a poor bunch eight months later.

The advance north continued and we were getting very near to the Yalu River, the border between Korea and Mongolia. It was then we had a very important casualty. It was the Company Commander, Major Apple. From the start, this

82 · PLUCK UNDER FIRE

officer had treated the war in Korea as a Boy Scout Jamboree. He was not alone in this attitude. Service in Africa, Italy and Normandy, and other places in World War Two had created an impression that warfare in the Post War years were just small skirmishes and hardly worth a mention in letters home. The Major never gained the respect of his men because of his contempt of our natural fears. Especially in the early months, we never actually knew where we were and were never told the intentions of our commanders.

Questions asked of the Major were met with a stock reply, "Your guess is as good as mine" and this said with a sarcastic smile. Obviously he did know more than the rank and file but made no attempt to calm our anxiety. On this particular day, we were roving over the hills and it wasn't until the evening that we heard that the Major had been sitting in his Bren gun carrier with one leg dangling over the side. His driver had to scrape by an American tank on a narrow road and the Major's leg was badly crushed. He was taken to a field hospital to the rear and that was the last we saw of him.

His place was taken by a Captain from the regiment and this officer had been awarded the Distinguished Service Order in Burma while still a Lieutenant. A D.S.O. awarded to a subaltern means it was a close run thing to a Victoria Cross. Notwithstanding, the Captain appeared to be a rather aloof person who considered his appointment as a strictly temporary affair, which it was. While he was with us there were three events for which I remember him. The first involved short rations. For a time we had to share one box of 'C' rations between two men. It was reported that on the first day of the shortage, Captain Blackberry had said to the Company Sergeant Major, "It's all right for the men to share a box of rations but I must have a box to myself!" We poor soldiers were disgusted with this appearance of selfishness but, forty seven years later, I had to admit to myself that the Captain was right. Like the Captain of a ship, he had to stand by himself if he was to command in good order.

We were still continuing the advance north and one stop was made on the rim of an earth wall that had surrounded a long gone city. The wall was about twenty feet high and twenty yards wide at the base. The construction must have taken years and used up all the earth for miles in every direction. The natural replacement of the earth seems to have taken place satisfactorily, so I presume the wall was some thousands of years old. Captain Blackberry ordered his Company Headquarters' staff to make a cross section cut into the wall to see what could be found from very ancient times. This work was carried on for two days at the expense of some very hard labour by some very disgruntled signallers and batmen, but nothing was found. With all the digging we had to do, I thought the extra workload was rather unfair but with hindsight I think the Captain was right again. There could have been some amazing discovery.

Jumping forward a bit, we were engaged in the retreat from the Yalu River, and I was leading my section on a very long and weary hike. The Captain, for some reason, fell in alongside me and we marched in step for a considerable length of time. We had bits of conversation on this and that but I had an uncomfortable feeling I was being tested – but for what I don't know. Forty seven years later, I met the Captain at a veterans' reunion. He was a Colonel retired and was a tiny, frail old man. His mind though was razor sharp. He reminded me of that walk together and then said he thought I was amazingly fit. I felt complimented, but I still don't know the reason for that march together.

Going back again in time, and still advancing north, the Company paused beside an abandoned village. Abandoned that is except for one old man. He seemed anxious to curry favour and kept pointing to the rear of one of the houses. I and a couple of others went to have a look see. A pit had been dug and into this pit were thrown hundreds of pairs of boots. An attempt had been made to cover over the boots but then the work was stopped. The boots were all brand new from the factory and were of leather with a sort of rubber sole. Most importantly though they were lined with fur. The old man wanted us to root through this find so he could take his share later and then blame the loss on the invaders. For a Korean in the dead of winter these boots were beyond price.

Naturally, we Westerners could not bear touching anything that came from the unclean Easterners but I thought I would have a look. I selected a pair that would fit me and hung them over my back by the laces. Three weeks or so later those boots were beyond price. They were perfect for slipping on at night for sentry duty. Far superior to the British Ammo boots for keeping the feet warm. Sadly I threw them away at the end of January 1951. Two months too early as it turned out. I only hope the old man was happy that winter. Good luck to him. He made me happy for many cold nights. The fur by the way was of oxen or maybe dog. Certainly not ermine or sable. Now I come to think of it, they were simply the hide of some animal turned inside out. Very effective though.

Eventually we went north until we reached the nearest position that our battalion was to get to the frontier. The weather was now icy cold but remained dry. One night I was snuggled down with my partner under one blanket and one groundsheet when I sleepily felt extremely comfortable. The sentry woke me for my turn on watch and I was very annoyed with him. I wanted to stay where I was forever. Struggling out of my feather bed comfort I felt and saw the reason for my sleepy pleasure. A foot of snow had fallen since I had got down to sleep and naturally everything under the snow was warm, warm, warm. On top of the snow though it was icy cold – a cold that was going to get worse with no let up until the middle of February. We commenced a period of three months where everything was frozen solid, day and night.

On this same day we witnessed an example of the Americans' attitude for the care of the troops in the front line. Some U.S. Engineers were working on a bridge nearby when a truck drew up loaded with overcoats. Although we cast an envious eye on the cargo it just wasn't practical for we British to don any more clothing. What followed now though was a real eye opener.

"Hey, you guys! How many of you are there?"

"Thirty I guess!" came the reply.

"O.K. Here's your overcoats."

Upon which three bundles were tossed into the snow and the truck roared off. Each bundle contained ten overcoats in different sizes. The G.I.'s came forward at their leisure and selected their size. I rather think there were only twenty nine G.I.'s in the party as one coat remained in the snow.

This incident would simply have never happened in the British Army that I knew. Each platoon would be lined up and Number, Rank and Name noted on a form. Each soldier would sign the form as a receipt and would receive a warning about returning the article in good condition in due course. Shells, bombs, grenades, bullets, trenches, snow, ice and other impediments would not be an excuse for failing to return the coat in good order.

Before we actually started retreating, there were a couple more incidents that really brought home the atmosphere of war. On the last hill that we went up while still facing the enemy, there was a call for men who had served in the Assault Pioneer Platoon in Germany.

These men specialised in the laying and clearing of mines amongst other things. My partner, Private Sprout, was one of these and off he went with some others under the direction of a Sergeant. He returned a couple of hours later in a state of shock. The party were lined up across the road in front of the battalion position and slowly went forward prodding the ground with their bayonets in a search for mines. They didn't find any, but it was rather an unnerving experience. It is one thing to do it in training, but in real life quite another! Furthermore, the mine clearing party had to advance over unknown territory towards the enemy. I felt a little jealous at the time as they went further north than the rest of us. It was from that position that we actually started going back the way we came.

While I say we started retreating, it was a couple more days before we actually heard of what was going on. In the meantime, we went up yet another hill covered in forestry. The enemy had dug some slit trenches on the ridge but had been driven off by American Point 155 medium artillery. There were some bodies scattered around and mostly lying face down. I knew they were dead but I fired some rounds from my Sten gun into the backs anyway. It was just in case some were faking, but also to give me some Dutch courage. I needed to prove myself to my men and show them that a little callousness was required all round.

One body though was a little different to the rest. The poor chap had dug down sufficiently to allow him to sit down with his legs stretched before him and his arms resting on the sides as though he was in an armchair. Then a shell landed nearby and he no longer had a head on his shoulders. Anyway, the bodies were thrown down the forward side of the hill, facing the enemy, and we settled down for the night.

Although we all had plenty of sleeping time, it was interrupted every thirty minutes by the Yanks. A Point 155 fired one shell over the ridge every half an hour. The missile was fairly close to the ridge in passing and the blast effect gave us a terrific thump in the stomach. We would be fast asleep then find ourselves coiled up in a ball. Slowly we would unwind ourselves, go back to sleep and then "Wham!" it all started over again. The knowledge that it was our own shells was no comfort and each shell was one more step in the process that leads to Combat Fatigue.

CHAPTER TWELVE

The Great Retreat

The War had been going great for General McArthur and the politicians of all countries involved. Several small patrols had actually reached the Yalu River and dipped their fingers in the icy waters. Then the Chinese launched a vast army across the river and the Allies had no option but to retreat. I don't pretend that as a Corporal I knew all the goings on between the Heads of States, or even that of the Colonels and Majors, but I did try to find out a little more than the very sparse information given to Tommy Atkins.

Really, the only method was to read the American Army newspapers which were superb for their purpose. One in particular was produced every day and was usually in our hands the day after publication. The editors always but always had a map on the front page showing the position of the front line. Sometimes we were told by our own officers the name of a town that we passed through and, by a bit of detective work, I was usually able to pinpoint our position to within twenty miles or so.

Why I had to do this I don't really know. It seemed important at the time, but I was certainly a loner in this respect. Most of the regiment could not place us within sixty or seventy miles of a given spot, and most of the regiment just did not care.

Even among the Regulars there was a feeling that we had been there quite long enough. While the National Servicemen, quite naturally, had not volunteered in the first place. There was an exception though to this lack of incentive to fight for King and Country. Private Pea was a National Serviceman of nineteen years of age and had led a very sheltered life. He was brought up as an only boy among six elder sisters – and it showed. He spoke very little and, of course, never boasted of imaginary conquests among the fair sex. Like me, he must have amazed at the daily outpourings of the others describing numerous sexual exploits.

Private Pea, however, was of a very different character in other respects. He was short, like me, but extremely tough. All during the rest of the campaign he was a most reliable fighting soldier. Whenever I led the way in an advance or took out a patrol, Private Pea was always the man at my back or by my side; and this without saying a word. Unworldly, shy and tongue tied, but a man among men. Once he got into an argument with Private Beetroot, who was boastful, foul mouthed and crude. Beetroot challenged Pea to a fight. Beetroot was dealt with and given a bloody nose in about three seconds. Nobody took liberties with Pea ever again.

When we really got started on the retreat and, of course, with our backs to the enemy, we had to pass through a long valley. This valley had high sloping sides but were of very even, grassy lawn like appearance. The top of each ridge was covered in trees and bushes but beneath this tree line a detachment of South Korean troops had been ordered to dig in and cover our retreat. The work had been going well and there were slit trenches going from one end of the valley to the other – about eight hundred yards. I don't know what the South Koreans had been told but when they saw the head of our column appear over the pass and facing south there was the most amazing reaction. The two nearest groups of four or five men on either side of the valley promptly abandoned their positions and ran down to the road. They left behind equipment, bedding and weapons. When the next nearest group saw what was going on they did the same, and so on down the line. As we marched on hundreds of South Korean soldiers were running down the slopes with only the kit they were wearing, hitting the road and then running south. It is just possible that the South Koreans did not recognise us as friendly troops, although we were all wearing the same American combat clothing as were the South Koreans.

At this point I must mention the refugees. All during the advance north we encountered refugees and I for one was rather puzzled. We never overtook any refugees going north but instead passed them as they were fleeing south. When the Chinese entered the conflict, hundreds of thousands of North Koreans clogged up the roads going south. There was a continuous stream of refugees day and night without let up. Now that I am older and wiser, I realise that the Koreans had no reason to trust the Chinese. Only five years before the Koreans formed part of the Japanese Army of Occupation in China and elsewhere. Even though they were now fellow Communists old hatreds die hard. The average Korean peasant only knew that a centuries old enemy was at his door and was taking no chances.

From experience, the Koreans knew that an invasion by Westerners did not mean wholesale rape and pillage but rather handouts and help; and so, they fled south from the absolute certainty of mayhem from soldiery of their long time enemy.

Equally, the Chinese had no reason to look kindly on the inhabitants of a country they had long feared and detested. In any event, they were all Communists and their first credo was – TRUST NO ONE! In one respect, the absence of the villagers made it easier for my regiment when foraging for creature comforts. Especially wood for which there was a constant demand. Doors, floors and partitions all went to give us the preservation provided by fire. We simply could not survive twenty four hours without heat of some kind, and our 'C' rations would remain frozen and uneaten. The Officers, of course, never took part in this foraging but relied on their batmen to provide a fire. Naturally, awkward questions were never asked.

Now and again we actually slept in the native dwellings but, for obvious reasons, not often.

You can't observe the enemy from a valley floor in the same way as you can from the top of a hill. In addition, we all felt rather squeamish about residing in a dwelling which normally housed perhaps twenty persons of all ages in two rooms and with no water and no toilet facilities, and which was fastened shut for five months of the year. The manner in which we existed for eight months would probably make the average Korean feel very squeamish indeed, but there we are – East is East, etc., etc.

Once during the bug out we fetched up at a very modern schoolhouse with a parquet floor. The whole company eagerly bedded down on the very hard floor, glad to have a roof over their heads. My partner and I were the last to arrive at this haven, and took a look at the mass of bodies stretched out without room to pass a piece of paper between two individuals. We very wisely went outside and found a piece of ground that was covered with snow on top of cinders. We bedded down and slept the sleep of the smug and self satisfied.

On another occasion we occupied a small deserted hamlet. Only a small contingent of the platoon wanted to sleep in the cottages but this included the Platoon Commander. During the night a fire was kept going in the kitchen at one end of the building. Like nearly all Korean cottages there was only one fireplace on which the food was cooked by boiling in pots. To conserve the heat, the chimney ran underneath the dwelling and emerged by way of a proper outlet which ran up the far end and dispersed the smoke into the air. As we discovered, this underfloor heating was super efficient. During the night, the lads on sentry kept the fire going all through the thirteen hours of darkness. At dawn we others found the doors open wide and the occupants tearing off their clothes rather than putting them on. Only one person was still rolled up in his bedding and that was Lt. Plumb. Eventually, he arose complaining of the heat and took up his blanket. The last to be taken up was his groundsheet and that was found to be smoking. Half of the sheet had actually burnt away. There was a lot of joking about that, but it certainly explained Lt. Plumb's capacity for sleep under all conditions. I might observe at this time that Lt. Plumb never, ever got up during the night to visit the sentries or for any other reason. Neither did the Platoon Sergeant. The Corporals ran the Platoon for thirteen hours in twenty four, and for most of the other hours as well.

There was one incident during this period which rather puzzled me at the time, and has intrigued me ever since. As usual, we had spent the day up a hill facing towards the enemy and then suddenly we got the order to get down to the road and wait for further orders. We were also told to get down that hill in a blazing hurry, which we did. My Company formed up in a single line on the far side of the road, and it so happened that I was facing a track coming down another hill and running down this track was a Platoon from another Company. I saw the Platoon Commander hit the road and immediately push off south. He never turned around to check on his men but merely shouted, "Come On!" Several men followed in a hurry and then came a Corporal with a very tense look on his face. He was a Rifle Section Commander, and I expected to see eight or nine others behind. There were only three, but the Corporal just forged his way south without a backward glance. It was now dark and then I heard several men calling out from up the track, "Hey! There's a man hurt up here!"

The Platoon Commander may not have heard, but the Section Commander was as near to the shouts as I was. He never stopped, but just went on. Leaving my men, I went up the track and found a group of four Private Soldiers around another chap on the ground. They were all young and obviously National Servicemen. The chap lying down gasped out, "I've broken my leg."

It was also obvious to me that I had arrived just in time. The other four were about to abandon their comrade to the Chinese who were supposedly only minutes away. I also noticed the casualty was a heavily built man, and it was going to be difficult getting him down the hill. First I took his rifle and threw it in the direction of the enemy. The National Servicemen gasped. Throwing away a rifle? It was unheard of in the British Army. Next I stripped off all his equipment and threw that after the rifle. Then the casualty shouted, "Just a minute! There's a pen and pencil set in my pack. It's a present from my girlfriend." Somewhat exasperated, I went to the pack and rooted out the present and gave it to the love struck Private. Then I selected the biggest of the other four to carry the casualty. We got him draped across the mule's back and away we went. On arriving at the road, I was pleased to see a Jeep. We dumped Mr. Broken Leg in the back but the driver wasn't happy.

"This is the Company Commander's Jeep!"

I told him the man had a broken leg and would have to stay where he was. I instructed the other four to find their Company and I rejoined my Section. Months later I found out that the casualty had been evacuated to Japan but not a word came back to me from any Officer or NCO from that Company by way of thanks. Perhaps they were fearful of exposing their own lack of leadership.

Months later in Hong Kong Private Broken Leg came back from Japan. He did not rejoin his own Company but was posted to mine. With some embarrassment, he thanked me for saving him from the Chinese but thereafter reverted to his true character. Apparently he had some experience in the boxing ring and constantly went around thumping smaller chaps, including me, to provoke a retaliation. Not a nice chap at all and his behaviour, which reeked of guilt, made me wonder about that broken leg – and why did his own Company not want him back?

In another incident during the Great Retreat we had spent the night on a very low ridge. This was unusual as our betters went by the motto, "The higher the hill the better!" and I suppose they were correct in this attitude. The higher we climbed, the higher the enemy had to climb in order to find us. Quite often though the enemy simply carried on past us and left us behind. Then we in turn ran into an ambush. Anyway, on this particular day we were cheerfully loading ourselves up for the forthcoming march when two mortar bombs landed in the company area. We didn't have any warning and five men were wounded. One of the wounded was a Lance Corporal who I barely knew. He suffered a not very serious wound in the arm, but went off to Pusan for shipment to Japan.

While waiting in the transit camp, he joined a bunch of GI's who were intent on touring the brothel area. The whole lot were picked up by American Military Police and shipped back to their units on the grounds they were now medically fit to resume their duties. The Lance Corporal took it all in good part, but he had forfeited his chance to avoid any further warfare. Lo and behold, a fortnight later he was slightly wounded once more. He was duly shipped off to Pusan again, but this time he never returned. He was now a much wiser man.

CHAPTER THIRTEEN

More Retreating

Like the Retreat From Moscow, our Retreat had the same two opponents. General Winter and General Mud. The cold at first was not so intensive and the Mud not so extensive but, nonetheless, these elements were there; and when the human body is in constant combat with these two Generals it can be very demoralising.

Easily the worst day so far was the one when we made a long haul lying on the baggage contained in the trailer of a Jeep. The Yanks, especially the Mortar Battalion, had an enormous number of Jeeps each of which pulled a trailer. As I only saw a small number of men during the day, I don't actually know how the Officers travelled, but the best of luck to them anyway. Starting at about nine a.m. three men were allocated to each trailer and told to sit atop the baggage over which was stretched a tarpaulin. It was bone breaking cold already, and we had no idea how long the journey was going to take. At first we sat upright but the icy wind forced us to lie down at full length on the baggage to try and gain some protection.

We also had to tuck our weapons under the ropes to avoid losing them. Our hands were so cold we could only hold on to something, **anything,** to avoid being thrown off. For long periods we went at a fair old speed. My two companions and myself lay on our backs and linked arms. The two outside men held on to ropes or anything so that we remained on board – and all the time the freezing Arctic blast from Siberia went on without let up. It was cold, cold, cold and we were miserable. Now and then there was a stop when we rolled off the trailer and stamped up and down to try and restore the circulation in our legs. Actually, we never succeeded in doing this. Our legs from the knee down remained without feeling for over twelve hours, and only partly thawed out over the next eight!

As one example of how cold it was, I will tell of my pile cap. The headwear was now an American winter combat cap. It had woollen piling inside, like a carpet, and which also covered two flaps which hung down over the ears. The flaps could also be buttoned underneath the chin forming quite a lot of protection. In the hurry of the morning, I failed to button up my flaps. That failure caused me a lot of grief. Despite repeated attempts, I was never able to get those flaps fastened. My fingers were just hard, blunt sausages with no mobility.

Funnily enough, I can't remember that we ever stopped for a meal and neither did we suffer thirst. Our water bottles were already frozen solid, but we never had to boil down snow to get some relief. Sometimes though, the convoy moved so slowly we were able to walk alongside the Jeeps for a couple of miles at a time. Never though did our legs and feet thaw out. That was one miserable day.

At long last it ended at about nine p.m. and we started marching onwards. All of a sudden we saw a glorious sight ahead of us. It was a huge blazing fire. The Colour Sergeant had travelled first in his truck and then collected a mass of wood and lit the bonfire. Everybody could not get around the fire together and so we took it in turns to stand at the warm glow for about ten minutes. The effect was more on our morale that on our bodies, but all of a sudden we were chattering and laughing. Even so, there was only one other day and night that was considered equally miserable and, even more, colder. That I will describe later.

My Company on this day never actually noticed where we were going except it was south. Without knowing it, we actually went past the capital of Pyongyang by way of the now infamous Kunuri Pass. A whole book has been written on this episode alone of the Korean War, but I will confine my remarks to the Regiment. As a disaster, the Kunuri Pass was monumental and thousands of Yanks lost their lives, thousands were wounded and thousands more were taken prisoner over four days. All the other Allied armies were also involved but, by a stroke of luck, my regiment went through first and missed the encircling hordes of Chinese; not that we entirely got away Scot Free as we returned twice to give a hand where required.

The day after the long haul, we went back on foot towards the Pass. Actually, we never really left the Pass as the valley through which the road ran was about ten miles long. The part which we considered the danger point was a bottleneck only about a hundred yards wide. As we were to discover right away, thousands of Chinese had avoided this bottleneck by going through the hills on either side to set up ambush points miles further south. Our first intimation that all was not well was the sight of a stationary Jeep containing the bodies of the driver and two Colonels of the U.S. Army. The vehicle was not on the road but on a Paddy Field about thirty yards away. The occupants had died by way of firearms being pushed through the open sides, which meant the killers were standing alongside the Jeep and also they were still very close to hand.

I found a Chinese water bottle that had been left behind by accident, but this also meant the enemy had been resting for some time before the shooting. The water bottle I kept for myself. It had a wide mouth and was sealed by a metal cap. Metal upon metal meant there was minimal moisture to freeze and indeed that water bottle never did freeze up even in January. The British 1944 Pattern equipment also had a wide mouthed water bottle sealed with a screw metal cap, but we did not have that equipment in Korea. Our water bottle was the 1937 Pattern – narrow mouthed and sealed with a cork. Utterly useless in Siberian conditions.

This seems a good opportunity to gripe about the equipment we were using at that time. Although the 37 pattern was not too bad for general purposes, it was made of webbing that had to be blancoed and the metal fixtures were made of brass which had to be polished. On the other hand, the 44 pattern was jungle green in colour and required no blanco. The metal fixtures were gun metal design and required no polishing. The 44 pattern when introduced was immediately more popular with the troops, but the War Office decreed it was designed for jungle warfare only. The 44 pattern was far more costly and, in addition, the 37 pattern was produced in enormous quantities during World War Two. Warehouses over the surface of the world were bulging with the stuff and so troops in various places such as Hong Kong had to make do with the old tried and trusted equipment in the cause of economy, which was the reason we carried around frozen water bottles.

But as I was saying, we went back up the Pass for the purpose of forming a rear guard and allowing the Yanks some relief from the constant attention of the Chinese hordes. On this particular day my Company, as usual, were allocated a hill to climb. The path was treacherous indeed with loose stones and roots to snare a careless foot. Sheer drops on one side made it extremely dangerous to fully laden men. I for one though was very surprised to find that we were not the first on that hill. A section of the battalion Medium Machine Guns were already in position. A machine gun breaks down into three main pieces for the purpose of movement but, even so, each part is very heavy. In addition, there is the ammunition and the water can for cooling the barrel. I was in awe of the tremendous effort that must have been made to get those guns set up and ready to fire. My Company's particular task was to provide protection for the Medium Machine Guns as well as to watch out for the enemy.

After digging the customary slit trenches and for a change finding it rather easy, we settled down for a quiet day. There was just one interruption and that was made by the Commanding Officer of the Battalion. It was the first sight of our C.O., Lt. Col. Peach, for most of us in 'C' Company and also one of mild surprise. The C.O. was not wearing the American Combat Clothing. Apparently he insisted on wearing British Battledress as his top layer of clothing. How he kept warm I do not know, but he certainly stood out in a crowd. The khaki colour was easily spotted among all the olive green. He also wore his forage cap and carried his cane. For all that, we instantly recognised him as a real fighting soldier, and one worthy of respect.

While he was still with us, I had borrowed Lt. Plumb's binoculars and was watching the progress of 'A' Company going up yet another wooded hill further up the Pass. 'A' Company were actually nearer the enemy than ourselves, but no sighting had yet been made of the Chinese. Suddenly, I saw them! Three

Light Machine Gun teams had appeared over the top of the hill being ascended by 'A' Company who were completely unaware of the enemy presence.

The distance between the Chinese and 'A' Company was as yet about six hundred yards but the Company continued to climb up towards certain death. I yelled a warning to the C.O. and other Officers about what I saw and instantly the C.O. had a look through his binoculars. Unfortunately for me, the Chinese were now motionless and invisible. The C.O. believed me if not the other officers. He grunted to his runner and his wireless operator, "Come on!" and the three went off down the forward slope, across the valley floor, and up the hill towards 'A' Company. The individual members of 'A' Company could not be seen with the naked eye, even when moving, but the C.O.'s progress up the hill was easily kept track of. His khaki stood out among the trees and bushes and the olive green. I saw him reach the head of the column and then shots were heard. The whole of 'A' Company then descended the hill again and reformed up on the road. No further effort was made to go up that particular hill. A very wise decision. Casualties would have occurred for no purpose. At least we now knew where the Chinese were, if nothing else!

The rest of the day for 'C' Company was uneventful until we got the order to get down the hill and retire once more for the night. The actual order though caused some astonishment. We were to run down that very dangerous track and form up in the order of march in **TEN MINUTES!** Nobody but nobody could achieve such a feat without some broken bones but anyway the Company tried. For me and my section though there was an added complication. It was getting dark but our Company Commander had spotted that the M.M.G. section had left behind two boxes of ammunition. He yelled at Lt. Plumb, "Take care of that Ammo!". Lt. Plumb then yelled at me, "Take care of that Ammo!" and went off down the track.

I looked at the boxes with some dismay. I knew only too well how much the boxes weighed, and it would take two men just to lift them off the ground. Negotiating those boxes down the track would take an hour at least, and it was almost dark. I was equally certain that Lt. Plumb would not hold up the transport back to our base for the sake of nine of his men. I told four of my chaps to lift up the boxes by the carrying handles, and then I fussed around until Lt. Plumb had disappeared. Me and my section were all alone with the Ammo. I ordered the boxes be thrown into a slit trench and then covered up with soil. This was done and only then did we make our way down the track. Lt. Plumb was waiting on the road and asked about the boxes. I replied, "We dealt with them!" He looked at me with a puzzled expression but made no further comment.

We were all taken back to our base to await another day, and that particular day, and the one after, were very eventful indeed.

CHAPTER FOURTEEN

Even More Retreating

On the morning following the Ammo incident my Company set off by foot for the Pass once more. I have no idea if the other companies were involved that day but I presume they were. As it happens, I was never to find out. We had been marching some hours but, with the state of the road and the enormous flood of Americans coming the other way, progress was slow. Not all the Yanks were demoralised by the way. Quite a number were in a jovial mood as they trudged south out of danger. I don't remember seeing one single Yank carrying any equipment, and quite a number were without firearms. To their credit, there did not appear to be any junior officers in the big bug out but we did see a couple of Colonels making their unaccustomed way on foot. At least they were rather shame-faced.

We also, as British troops, became aware that the Yanks liked to have actual proof that they had been under fire. Word of mouth was not good enough. Without actually suffering bullet wounds, there sprang up a practise that would suffice for the non-combatants in rear. The American helmet comes in two parts. The outer steel cover and a softer thinner liner which touches the skull. American troops on peace keeping duties in places like Germany usually only wear the liner which is brightly painted. In Korea, and once in a safe area, it was standard practise to take off the steel outer cover, place it on the ground, and then fire a bullet at the side. If it was carefully done, then only a dent would appear. Some clowns though fired the bullet head on which made a hole clean through. How they explained why the inner liner remained undamaged is not clear. Of course, so many did this trick to gain a badge of honour that very soon no one was believed, and the practise died out.

We had been marching a couple of hours towards the Pass and the enemy when I was suddenly taken out of the column and given instructions to report to a Lieutenant of the American Army. The Lieutenant was in charge of a Motor Pool a short distance away. My Company marched off and I never saw them again for twenty four hours. What the Company did in that time I have no idea. I never asked and nobody volunteered any information, but perhaps our experiences when we did meet rather overshadowed everything else.

When I did find the Lieutenant I noticed two things. One, he was the most perfect physical specimen of a human being I had ever seen. He was built like a Greek God! Two, he was the only white man there. Everyone else was coloured. That situation did not bother me, but then I was unaware of the vast social gulf between whites and coloureds in the American way of life. Perhaps my ignorance was just as well. In any event, I was treated with courtesy and kindness by all and sundry. Having been shown a tent where I was to spend the night alone, I was taken by the Lieutenant to where four trucks were parked side by side. While the drivers stood by, the Lieutenant explained that these four trucks were for my use only. They would be ready to move off at seven a.m. the next day – the purpose being to pick up my Company and bring them back to the base. The Lieutenant also assured me that he would be there at seven a.m. to see me on my way. He strode off and I never saw him again.

Something was niggling at the back of my neck. Why was I chosen for this task? I could not drive and I knew nothing about Motor Transport. I had a flash of inspiration however. I got out a piece of paper and wrote down the numbers of the trucks. What a wise decision that turned out to be. For the remainder of the day I relaxed, which was a huge treat. No climbing hills or digging slit trenches or standing sentry-go. For the life of me, I can't now remember what I did for food on that particular day, which is strange considering that food was the priority in our thoughts. I certainly remember queuing up at the kitchen the next morning for chow and being the sole object of attention for a while. I thought it was because I was British, and maybe it was, but I now realise it was because I was a white man intruding on forbidden territory. In any event, there was no animosity but curiosity aplenty.

After breakfast I donned my full regalia and went looking for my transport. My heart sank! There was no sign of my trucks. I started a search. I found one truck, with driver, at the back of the dining tent. The driver explained it was for camouflage purposes in case of an air raid. I got into the passenger seat and we drove back to the assembly point. I didn't give the driver any more instructions as I thought my intentions were quite obvious. I found the next truck parked between two rows of tents used for living quarters. I did not ask for any explanation, but got the truck back to the assembly point only to find the first truck had vanished again. I told my second driver very firmly to stay where he was. It took a long time, but I eventually got all four trucks together at the departure point.

All four drivers now gathered together at the front of the column. They looked at me and I looked at them. Then one cheerful rogue announced, "Hey you guys! I'm going to get me some chow!" I swung my Sten gun at waist level and pointed the muzzle at **their** waists. I announced, "We are leaving!" I was just angry enough to actually open fire. The cheerful one then suddenly said, "OK. Let's go!"

All four drivers went to their trucks and started up. I got into the passenger seat of the lead vehicle and away we went. Surprisingly, the other three followed on. I had no idea how far I had to go but had been told to keep going until I found the Company. This was no particular problem as there was only the one road. We went on for some miles and, at one point, forged through a wide but shallow stream. The drivers went through the water very, very slowly, but I had no knowledge of why at the time.

We had left the base at nine o'clock instead of seven, and our journey was spread over about ten miles. It was something like midday when we met the Company on the way back on foot. I fully expected a right roasting for being so late, but not a word of reproach was said. Instead, the officers seemed rather surprised to see me at all. The trucks were turned round at a small clearing, and the troops loaded. There were more than four officers with the Company, but I felt I had a right to a seat in the cab of the leading vehicle, and duly asserted my place. Nothing was said. On my left, as we were now facing south, was yet another hill. On my right was a large stretch of paddy fields going back at least a mile before meeting another range of hills. Technically though we were still in the Pass.

I must also mention that the flood of retreating Americans had now ceased except for one or two stragglers. I had thought we could pick some up on the way back, but it was not to be. My driver had only just got moving when I saw out of the corner of my right eye a line of puffs in the paddy field and, at the same instant, there was a clang underneath my seat and a cracking of wood above. We had been hit by a burst of fire from about two hundred and fifty yards away. I had never noticed until now that the driver and passenger on these trucks actually sit on the petrol tank which forms a bench going from one side to the other. Seats are placed on the flat top. I also noticed straight away there was a stream of petrol pouring out on to the road from a position a few inches from my backside. One bullet had put a hole in the tank and another had smashed into woodwork at the back and above and gone through a corporal's arm. Of course, as soon as the troops had sat down, out came the fags. I leant out of the cab and yelled, "Put out the cigarettes!" Two squaddies looked at me as though I was mad, and then they saw the stream of petrol. There was a scramble to put the fags out.

This whole incident only took a few seconds, but my driver had not noticed a thing. In my best cool, calm and collected voice, I said to him, "You had better go a little faster!" He looked at me rather puzzled. Then another burst of fire went straight across in front of the windscreen, and this time he heard the cracking sound. His face went from black to grey and he put his foot down. For ten miles, without stopping, we went as fast as possible considering the state of the road and the odd group of Korean refugees. We hit the stream and a wall of water came up and over, drenching everyone in the back. Eventually we came to a stop and the troops got down. The wounded corporal was taken away and also a wounded sergeant of the U.S. Army who had been picked up by the Company. He had been crawling along the road for two days and nights, but had been ignored by his comrades.

Never though was there such a transformation in a human being as that undergone by my driver. He was ecstatic! He was running around like a turkey who had been told that Christmas was cancelled. "Hey, look you guys! I got real bullet holes! Real Gook bullet holes!"

From the manner of his speech, I surmised that many an American truck went through the same treatment as that dealt out to the steel helmet. Grass was stuffed into the bullet hole in the "gas" tank and away went the trucks with three contented drivers and one delirious hero who had no more need of sham bullet holes.

I had no idea then and still haven't of what the rest of the battalion did on that particular day. This was not unusual though. It was very rare for one company to be dug in alongside another and it was even rarer for any type of communication to go on between my Company and another. After all, my Company had never met any of the rest of the battalion before Korea. In addition, that common meeting place, the N.A.A.F.I. canteen simply did not exist for us, and so we remained strangers until the regiment returned to Hong Kong.

At the end of the day, my own feelings were one of vast relief that I had completed the task that I had been given. The danger that we had undergone was only of secondary importance to me, but that is not to say that I was not afraid. I was, but the responsibility had taken the edge off the terror! I did rather feel at the time that the same officers who had detailed me for the task might now seek me out to express their thanks. It was not to be but, on the other hand, they were rather busy gathering up their men.

That day though seemed to set the tone for the rest of the Campaign. With time honoured tradition the junior officers were expected to make the rounds of the slit trenches to ask if all was well – even to make jokes, if required. That never happened with my Platoon. Once the orders had been given for the night, and usually relayed through the Platoon Sergeant, Lt. Plumb retired to a corner of a foreign field that was his alone. We would not see him again until the following day and, if we had no orders to move, not even then.

Although I may seem to be condemning Lt. Plumb for his failure as an officer, in reality I am giving an explanation for other moments of despair later in the Campaign. While many Private Soldiers failed to meet their obligations in times of stress, it was because they had no leader. When there should have been words such as, "Come on, chaps!" there was instead only silence. Even during the Campaign, I felt sorry for poor Lt. Plumb and have done so ever since. He was given a commission and delegated for a task for which he was utterly unsuited. The system it was that failed, but never will that be admitted.

I might also mention letters from home at this time. Mail, of course, was of paramount importance for all concerned. I didn't receive much mail, but that was due to a particular family problem, and has no bearing on this story. Others though were married or had girl friends and letters were eagerly received and read immediately, no matter what! In my youthful ignorance, I once interrupted Private Sprout, who was married, to pass on some instruction but was very angrily put in my place. That though set me thinking. Some of the men in the Company were barely able to read and write, if at all, and in typical fashion tried to cover up their lack of schooling. In these cases, some feelers should have gone out to enquire if anyone needed a hand to compose a letter home. As far as I was aware, no feeler was put out and, as a result, there were a number of very angry young men who showed no respect for their Officers and NCOs.

Funnily enough, it was these same illiterates who were the bravest in battle. They after all had something to prove.

CHAPTER FIFTEEN

Idle On Parade

After Kunuri and for the next two months my Company were never actually engaged in any fighting. There were a couple of scares and the other companies were involved but not 'C' Company. Perhaps it was just as well. If we had thought we had suffered hardship before, there was much worse to come. In my own opinion, a little light skirmishing would have concentrated our minds wonderfully on the danger and away from the exhausting discomfort.

In our gradual progress south there were a number of incidents that are worth mentioning if only because nobody else seems to have the courage to speak out. The first that comes to mind is the meeting up with some Turkish troops. The Turks as a nation has a fearsome reputation in battle and history bears out the facts. Our particular segment were a bunch of troops without a leader, arms, equipment or rations. When we first saw these troops we also heard the story of the Turkish battalion who were ordered to take a village, which they did. They also butchered every civilian man, woman and child in the process.

Many, many years later I learnt that the Turks did not have it all their own way in Korea and, in one particular brush with the Chinese, had suffered great losses. A number of Turks were taken prisoner but later released for reasons unknown. A small group were taken over by my regiment for the purpose of using them to show us where the Chinese were located. Nobody in the regiment spoke Turkish, and none of the Turks spoke English. It was my unfortunate lot to have a Turk allocated to my section. At no time was it ever suggested that the Turks were to be given rations, blankets or other equipment from battalion stores. We went through the day with the stray being fed by us but, of course, no dialogue took place. Came the night and, as usual, no officer or Sergeant wanted to know. Even the Company Commander walked away. The Turks having been found of no use for the purpose intended, they were simply abandoned.

In all humanity the Turks should have been sent to the rear for succour as soon as they were found, but now nobody would take responsibility. I found myself being obliged to ask my men for blankets for the Turk, but I could not do it. We only had one blanket each, and for three to share two blankets with the temperature below zero was to risk frostbite for all three. I ordered the Turk away, and I felt ashamed at the time, and still feel ashamed to this day. I also felt anger with my Platoon Commander and Platoon Sergeant who studiously looked the other way. The Turk found comfort with another Platoon, but my rage and shame still persists. Why, oh why, were the Turks not provided from our battalion stores! I was just beginning to realise that the whole regiment were petrified with fear of our Quartermaster. He simply would not provide the troops with a single button or one ounce of food more than the regulation entitlement – and we were at war!

The Turks may have been our Allies, but they were not on the Regimental strength and were to be given **nothing.** A strange fellow was the Quartermaster, and I believe he had been promoted beyond his capability, causing him to become mentally unbalanced. From beginning to end of our campaign the Quartermaster and his staff behaved as though we were merely on a training exercise, and even the casualties made no impression on their tiny minds.

On the 23rd November 1950 there occurred an American holiday called Thanksgiving. I can recall seeing Thanksgiving mentioned in several American films, but I had no idea what it represented, and still don't. The Yanks, on the other hand, had no idea that there were areas of the known world that did not celebrate Thanksgiving. They were amazed that the British had made no special preparations for this very important day. As a consequence, the battalion was given a special issue of Thanksgiving Turkey and other delights. We took it in turn to descend from our hill to take part in a really fabulous meal which included a **real** bread roll. This was our first taste of bread since arriving in Korea and it awakened taste buds long since forgotten. That bread roll was really, really delicious!

Another incident that occurred around this time was to be entertained by the 24th Division Orchestra. The war was still raging elsewhere, but we were marched from our slit trenches to a natural open air theatre. We sat on a rising bank of a hillside while below on a flat field was set out about thirty members of the orchestra, complete with music stands and a conductor. The cold was just bearable, but **only** just with gloves. The musicians played without any covering on their fingers and I felt sorry for them. For about an hour they gave us all the Songs of the Shows and other light opera. When it was over, we clapped politely and marched back to our trenches. That was the only live entertainment we had in eight months, but it was something of a mystery. Perhaps the Yanks thought it was the last opportunity to exercise their instruments before fingers and valves froze up forever.

Also at this time we were informed that the Regiment was being withdrawn from the Korean War Zone and returned to Hong Kong. I was myself very disappointed at the news. I had not yet been cured of War Fever and the desire to prove myself in battle. Curiously, the news was not received with rapture and cries of jubilation by the rest of the Company. I suspect the majority felt as I did – that we had not been given a fair chance.

Anyway, while we were waiting for orders, it was felt that the troops had to be kept occupied. A Football Competition combined with an Athletics Meeting seemed to be the answer. A very large expanse of paddy field was marked out with some white powder, and there was a football pitch in the middle, surrounded by a circular running track. We only had the clothing and the boots we wore and so it was not expected that we would break any records of any description. Two days after the news of the withdrawal, we were told the regiment was once more in the Order of Battle, and we moved further south yet again. Even the National Servicemen were silently relieved.

On one of the stops where it was fairly certain we would be there a couple of days, it was decided the Company needed a bath. A forty four gallon drum was split down the middle, and one half was supported on its side and a fire lit underneath. Water was added from a stream until it was nearly full. Men were called forth in fours and told to strip down and lay their clothes on their groundsheets. Towels, fresh socks and underwear had to be on hand. Four men got in and scrubbed down in a great hurry and then ran through the snow to their towels. Four more got in and then another four, by which time there was a thick scum on the surface of the water. I was in the next four and I cringed a bit when I saw the condition of the advert for Pears Soap, but I scrubbed down anyway. A mad dash followed to get dry and clothed before frostbite set in. Each time sixteen men went through the water was changed from the other half of the drum. Me and three others had drawn the short straw. Still, it was better than nothing, or so we were led to believe!

Up to then, and for the rest of our stay in Korea, I never observed an Officer or Sergeant going through any sort of washing or bathing process. I presume they did perform some sort of ablutions, but it was a well kept secret; though I never felt curious about their hygiene. It is only now that I wonder how the Officers and Sergeants managed. Ah well, on with the saga.

Another inspection occurred at about this time that enforced the suspicion that the lower ranks could not, or would not, look after themselves. A foot inspection was ordered. Despite going up hill and down dale for two months, and without a single enquiry from our officers about the state of our feet, it was deemed a foot inspection was required. In normal barracks procedure, and whenever the regiment had been on a route march, a foot inspection was carried out by the junior officers. If a blister was found, there was an automatic assumption that it was the soldier's fault for not marching properly, or not putting on fresh socks. In this inspection not one blister was found. I put this down to the fact that the foot was never exposed to the open air. I am probably wrong in this diagnosis, but it is a curious fact that the battalion's feet were never a problem in Korea – not even from frostbite, provided the feet were kept dry. The inspection revealed a hundred pairs of remarkably white and clean feet. That was our one and only foot inspection, but at about the same time we were issued with new boots if we said we wanted them. When I first joined the Army it was decided I was a seven large. I stuck to this size even though I grew another inch over the next year. Long, long before Korea, I found the leather crushing in my Achilles Heel causing some pain. I gladly upped to size eight small and never suffered again. A curious thing about the issue of boots was the lack of arched eyebrows. We just said we wanted new boots and we were given them. The Quartermaster must have gone temporarily sane.

While continuing to withdraw to the south, there were often times when we stayed in one place for a couple of days, but one morning we were saddled up when we were issued with one bottle of beer. I had never been a drinking man myself, and to go for two or three months without the taste of beer was not unusual, but now there was a problem. Did we carry the beer or drink it on the spot. I believe there was a hundred per cent in favour of drinking the beer there and then! The thought of the extra weight to be carried all day did the trick. I thought the taste of the ale, (Japanese), was appalling and it reminded me of my first pint at the age of eighteen. After the last two months of extreme exhaustion, our bodies had been cleansed of all noxious habits and I don't think there was a young soldier who did not think the same. Of course, there were the few canteen cowboys who had to pretend that the beer was delicious. If I remember rightly, I poured half of mine away. What was curious though was that the beer was not frozen. We had a couple of issues of beer over the next month or so and none of the bottles had to be thawed out. How did they do that?

Another Army tradition that was exercised at this time was Church Parade. Born and brought up a Roman Catholic, but with fits and starts at Mass attendance, I was not a great believer. My religious fervour had been blunted by my last Headmaster at a Catholic school. A sadist of the worst kind who took delight at not only beatings with the cane, but constant humiliation of his pupils. There wasn't a child at that school who was not highly delighted to see their fourteenth birthday. As a consequence, my attendance at Mass on a Sunday was a result of being ordered to attend. Korea though brought home to us that we ought to take out a form of insurance and so we attended Mass when one was available. The Roman Catholic Padre had to attend the needs of several units and so we saw him only a few times during the campaign, and **never** on top of a high hill! Neither did we see the Padre in the very depths of the cold, cold winter. If I recovered my faith slightly during the campaign, it was to lapse again for another forty years. These days, I am glad to report, I am no longer a lapsed Catholic and I feel better for my recovery.

During the whole campaign in Korea, ground troops were never in any real danger from enemy aircraft but, in the early days and after Kunuri, there had been an incident where aircraft operating from Manchuria had strafed some of the South Korean forces. This was the one and only time it happened, but Headquarters had to take notice, obviously, and so orders percolated down from the top. The first I knew of it was when Lt. Plum came to my position in a very agitated state. He ordered me to ensure that our slit trenches had overhead protection.

"Get on to it right now, Corporal!" he almost screamed at me with a wild and desperate look about him. I could swear he was actually trembling.

It so happened, we were in a very large valley and everywhere we looked we could see nothing but grass. There wasn't a tree or bush or any buildings, or even a fence of any description. Nothing at all that could be laid over the top of a trench to support more earth, but Lt. Plum insisted I started right away. I was flabbergasted, but I got my men to dig down another four inches. That was all that could be done but, being already exhausted, we were not pleased and Lt. Plum suffered a further loss of face.

CHAPTER SIXTEEN

Goodwill To All Men

After one or two more moves we finally crossed the 38th Parallel again and finished up in a place called Ouijongby; not that we ever actually saw a town by this name as we were once more out in the wilderness. The enemy, by all accounts, were a long way away and we were able to do some serious resting. My Company were in a narrow valley where there were lots of nooks and crannies and the earth was quite soft. I imagine that many ditches and moats and other fortifications had been constructed over the years as we had no trouble digging ourselves a bunker with overhead cover. My section constructed a sort of cave with a fireplace and straw covering the floor. During the day we all crammed into the cave and just talked. At least it was warm, if a trifle smoky. If anybody wished a couple or three men could stretch out and sleep there during the night, but nobody ever did. This atmosphere was too foul. In any event, we now had winter sleeping bags and were wonderfully warm in our pup tents. We became very complacent and sentry duty was performed in name only.

On most days there was an issue of beer and we even had access once to a N.A.A.F.I. wagon where extra supplies of cigarettes and chocolate could be bought, if we had any money, which we didn't! All in all though we were quite happy.

Christmas day came around in that valley and the Sergeants came round in the early morning with mugs of tea, this being the custom when in barracks. We also had a proper Christmas Dinner but eaten in a hurry because of the cold. By this time the Ladies of the Women's Voluntary Service in Middlesex had got around to knitting scarves and mittens and balaclavas for their "boys at the front". We were all extremely grateful for these extras as the Army never got around to issuing these badly needed items. The mittens especially were a godsend as one pair of ordinary woollen gloves were very inadequate at thirty below.

About the third day in our cave, the straw caught fire and we were in a very dangerous situation. We all scrambled out coughing and spluttering but without any casualties. We could easily have left the straw to burn itself out, but it was our "home" plus, of course, there was wood upholding the roof. One or two of us tried to pat out the flames but it was hopeless. Then Private Shamrock took hold of a groundsheet and dived into the cave holding the cape in front of him. He spread the cape right across the floor and actually put out the fire. A very gallant act for which the section was grateful. When we took up residence again the stench was awful, but we had nowhere else to go. If any other person in the platoon or even the company heard the commotion, they all kept their heads down and their bodies warm.

I think it was Boxing Day when the same Private Shamrock decided to take a trip to see the fleshpots of the Capital, Seoul. There were daily convoys going up and down the only road and Shamrock had no bother in hitching a lift. No one in command had ever suggested that we could leave the Company area and so it was taken for granted that we stay where we were.

Shamrock was away for one night and never spoke of his experience, but he seemed mildly satisfied. It may be a coincidence but from the time of his return we all had body lice. I later learnt from a pamphlet issued by the Yanks that lice come in three types. There are head lice, pubic lice and body lice. We had this last type and probably the most inoffensive. During the day the scourge seemed to lie very still but, come the night, we scratched and scratched, making sleep almost impossible. Later on I will describe how we got rid of the plague.

Jumping back a bit, I must mention the "Old Soldier". At the end of October we had posted to the Company a Lance Corporal who was fifty three years of age. He was assigned to assist the Colour Sergeant but spent most of his day huddled round a fire. At night he was bedded down in the Company truck and covered over with many blankets. Never should a man of his years be sent to serve in such atrocious conditions, but there was a purpose in the posting. Old Soldier had served in World War One and World War Two and possibly on the North West Frontier of India as well as Palestine. In any event, his campaign medals stretched over a lot of years. Somebody back at the Depot at Mill Hill, London, had correctly surmised that there would be a medal for Korea and thought it a good idea for Old Soldier to get yet another campaign medal showing his service to King and Country, stretching over a period of at least thirty eight years. Even for a General or a Major in the Royal Army Pay Corps this length of service is exceptional, but for a Lance Corporal in the Infantry, outstanding! It was almost certainly a correct guess that three months in Korea would be sufficient for a medal and Old Soldier lasted exactly that long. His departure is the subject of another story, but I will come on to that later. Nobody, of course, quite realised in October 1950 just how bad the winters were on the 38th Parallel, and sending Old Soldier was an act of Criminal Lunacy. I don't know what happened to Old Soldier on his return to Britain, but I would like to know. Was he perhaps put on display at the Regimental Museum?

On New Years day the Chinese opened up another offensive and once more we were on the road to the south. The weather by now was really bitterly cold, morning as well as evening. For my battalion it was just a matter of shuffling around on trucks and foot except for one particular day and night. We had finished up in a very small valley surrounded by massively high hills, if not actually mountains. There wasn't room for the whole battalion to bed down, and so my Company were sent up to a high ridge on the pretext of all round defence. We set off quite cheerfully as we had done this sort of thing so many times before.

Once we were on the knife edge though, we felt quite different. It was so, so cold that I cannot describe it. On top of that, the wind blasted across the top of the ridge making the chill factor even worse. There had been snow, of course, but this was now pure ice a couple of inches thick. We spread along the ridge and were told to dig in. A ludicrous suggestion as we all knew. The forward slope by the way was almost perpendicular! Any Chinese making an assault up there would have to use crampons and ropes. Nonetheless we had to make a start.

The first essential was to find a flat space upon which to lay our bedding which was once again a groundsheet and a blanket each. As usual our large packs and winter sleeping bag was placed in the Company truck along with the pup tents. We didn't even know where the truck was at this stage, and it certainly would not be within reach. Some of the clever dicks in the Company had become rather complacent of late, and rather expected to see the truck every night after a days march. As a consequence, a few had deposited groundsheet and blanket on the truck as well that morning. So much less to carry was the feeling. Now they had to face a terrible night with no bedding at all. Perhaps there should have been a little more supervision by the Officers and Sergeants, but we were all living a very desperate sort of life. Digging in commenced but all we were doing was chipping little slivers of ice from a solid surface which was as hard as concrete. Even so, my partner and I managed to clear a flat sleeping place about an inch and a half deep. It so happens we did better than most and our tools were still intact.

There came a cry from the other Platoon Commanders to which Lt. Plum made no objection. They were demanding that our Platoon hand over our picks and shovels as all the rest of the tools had been shattered. I think this was an act of deliberate sabotage. So futile was the ice breaking that the picks and shovels had been whacked down with all the strength of the owners. All the tools now had broken shafts and were useless. Why a demand was made on our platoon I don't know, but I think the other Lieutenants understood Plum only too well. I heard the commotion going on and told Sprout to lay out our groundsheets and blankets on top of our space. I then quickly hid our solid gold pick and shovel underneath. On top of that I piled our small packs and other equipment. The trick worked and we were not bothered by the plunderers. The funny part about all this was that I never saw any entrenching tools being used. I and Sprout still had ours slung from our webbing belts, but it never once crossed our minds to use them! For chipping ice they were ideally shaped, but they were entirely forgotten.

It was now night and all activity had ceased, but there was nothing around to make a fire. In addition, we were very, very hungry. Far below we could see fires going and figures flitting around the flames. Then came a bugle call that echoed loud and clear. It was "come to the cookhouse, boys!" We felt a rage of pure hatred towards our lucky comrades but, in due course, were sent a message to come down for our share of food. Everyone went down together so there was no worry about the Chinese hordes. The meal was magnificent and back up the ridge we trudged. Those of us who had a blanket and groundsheet laid them out in preparation for sleep. I don't remember any suggestion of sentries so probably there wasn't any intention for lookouts. Even though we couldn't do any more digging, it was midnight before we attempted to sleep. The cold was even more intense. For myself, I found sleep impossible. That mind snapping cold was sheer agony. Then I thought of something! On the way up, we had passed a wrecked building. The walls were made of proper bricks as we knew them in Britain. There were wooden doors and wooden joists, but the roof had fallen in. I was most interested in the walls as a shelter from the wind. It was now about 1am.

Without telling anyone, I made my way down to the refuge but I was not the first. Half a dozen others were already there and what's more, they had a fire going. Probably these others were the ones without a blanket. Anyway, they made room for me although not a word was spoken. I sat down with my back to a wall and was appreciative of the shelter and the heat. Within minutes I was asleep and stayed that way until dawn. The fire was out which meant my comrades in need had also slept somehow. I made my way back up to the ridge and asked Private Sprout how he had managed. "Fine!" he said. "I slept right through the night." I was amazed but then he did have two blankets and two groundsheets. Even so, he was lying on a sheet of ice. If anyone else noticed my arrival from far down below, not a word was said. In any case, keeping your nose out was becoming a feature of this campaign. No matter where you went or what you did, no questions were asked. Leaving the Platoon position without being ordered to meant you were on the scrounge, and the only interest was in what you brought back or what you had found.

We left the ridge that morning, and I can say without any doubt that was the worst day and night we had in Korea. It was sheer misery and so cold.

We now finished up in a factory alongside the only road in the area. The building was made of wood, but there were pieces missing from the walls and, although there were huge doors, they had large gaps top and bottom. The icy Siberian wind blew through like a banshee but still, it was shelter of a kind.

CHAPTER SEVENTEEN

All Quiet On Our Front

Once we had settled in for at least the one day in the factory, we immediately felt so much better. Anything was better than the icy ridges exposed to all weathers. As usual, the first thought was of wood and water. The water was no problem as the snow lay round about crisp and two feet deep. We just crushed the snow down in the section billy-can and put it on the fire. Our billy-can by the way was an item of extreme importance. It was a throw away can that formerly held U.S. rations and could boil up about three pints of water. Far better than each soldier boiling up his own water in a mess tin. I think it was my section that first adapted one of these cans by puncturing two holes at the side and threading through a piece of wire for carrying, but all the Company took the hint and then they became indispensable. Whenever we had to move, the last item to be picked up was the billy-can, but we never dared to leave it behind.

While I am on the subject of fires and heating up our 'C' rations, I must point out a couple of things that would no doubt horrify our Mothers and Nursing personnel. First, our fingers. With the adjustment of the fire and the stacking of cans around the same, our fingers became permanently black with soot and ashes and washing (infrequent) never removed the stain. Although heating up a can of beans and opening with the small can opener provided and then spooning out the contents avoided actual contact, the rest of the rations were all handled by our fingers. I never knew of any case of stomach ache from eating our rations. Another taboo item in most films and books is the matter of emptying our bladders and bowels. In minus zero temperatures both actions were something of a problem, not to say downright dangerous.

Urinating was not carried out in a light hearted manner, but rather of a carefully considered manoeuvre. First, the fingers of the right hand had to be warm. Then swiftly removing a glove which immediately exposed the fingers to the frost, a fumble was made to unzip the combat trousers then undo the buttons on the battledress trousers, then poke through the long johns to extract the member. While the waters flowed we prayed it would not take long. When finished, we buttoned up again with all haste but often with fingers growing swiftly numb. Defecating was an action that was left to the last possible moment. Removing the combat jacket and battledress blouse and exposing the braces which were then left dangling, all the zips and buttons were undone and we launched ourselves towards the chosen spot. Toilet paper was placed close to hand and then we lowered our clothing and stooped down. Bowels were emptied and paper used in no more than five seconds. The clothing was hitched up and we ran for shelter where the closing up was completed. There were never any washing facilities on hand – just the snow.

We had just one bath in January 1951 and changed our underclothes at the same time. That bath proved a godsend. Our nights were plagued by the body lice we were hosting ever since Private Shamrock had his fling in Seoul. It was scratch,

scratch, scratch all night. Somebody had decided that a bath might prove a cure. At one end of the factory there was a small room which contained a very large boiler heated by a fire underneath. I don't know who provided the water or the wood, but anyway we got started. We removed all our clothing except our underwear and remained by the section fire. At a shout from the boiler room we took it in turns to run twenty yards and into a burst of steam. Shedding the clothing and socks, we climbed up the small platform and stood in the hot water. At the same time a laundry man gathered up the discarded clothing and dumped it into a smaller vat which was bubbling hot. A couple of dumps up and down with a stick and the garments were thrown to one side.

We sluiced ourselves down with soap and not forgetting our hair stepped down from the boiler. Gathering up our clothes, we stepped outside stark naked. The garments were thrown over the snow and we ran back to our fire where we dried ourselves on our face towels in a hurry. I don't know how often the water was changed but it was already pretty murky when I got in. The question now was, had we got rid of the lice? The delightful answer was a glorious YES! Between the boiling and the freezing, the lice gave up. It took days to defrost and dry our clothing, but we were much happier for the rest of the campaign.

One constant requirement was wood to keep our fires going. Each section and Platoon H.Q. kept a fire going day and night within the walls of the factory. The factory itself was largely made of wood, but we had the good sense to leave well alone. Although the snow was driven through gaps and holes, and covered us during the night, at least the wooden walls and doors kept off the lower twenty degrees of frost. Instead, we had another source of wood close to hand. There was an abandoned village about one hundred yards away and all the dwellings had solid upright timbers, roof supports and wooden flooring. Over three or four weeks the Company demolished every house to extract the wood. It was a daily task of half of each section to venture out into the cold to fetch a supply. Of course, we did not just haul a daily ration but took back what we could carry and hoarded what was not used. The long thick uprights could not be chopped up and so we put one end on the fire and pushed it forward as it burnt through. Without those fires we simply could not have survived. At one time we had word that the President of South Korea was very displeased at the way villages were disappearing.

We held off for three days until our hoarded supply ran out and then went back to the village for more fuel. It was just as well we moved when we did as there was no wood left in that hamlet – just heaps of stone and mortar!

We did well for food as our 'C' Rations were delivered every day without fail and, considering the state of the roads, the American drivers did a really great job. Once, however, I was given a pack which appeared to be quite normal on the outside with the cardboard box in perfect order. On opening the lid, I discovered the cans had gone from about four and a half inches high to just one inch high. The result apparently of being parachuted from a plane. I am not a scientist so I can't explain why the cans did not explode sideways, sending the contents everywhere, but there it is. Anyway, I objected to the state of my carton but the Platoon Sergeant said it was probably alright. I suggested it would be impossible to heat up the tins and what about the tin which held the cigarettes, coffee, toilet paper, jam and cocoa – all impacted together! The Sergeant grumbled but had to go and fetch me another. Typical of the prevailing attitude of the Quartermaster and his Staff. The lowly soldier was expected to make do and mend. We actually made the best of everything for every hour of every day – but there were limits!

About half way through our stay at the factory, I was sent out on a liaison patrol to contact the Australians who were in a position between us and the Chinese, but nobody knew for sure where the enemy were located. I found the Aussies with a proper trench system all linked up together and with dugouts. They were just as cold as us though and kept well inside their shelters. Of course, the Aussies had no idea that anyone was coming to visit them and, after a few words, I returned to my own fire. Nobody was the least interested in what I had to report; it was just an exercise in order that my Company Commander could say he was keeping on his toes.

I might add that from that time on I led every single patrol that was ordered by the Company Headquarters. Night or day and for whatever reason I was the Patrol Commander and, of course, it was my men that I took with me. Not a Major, Captain, Subaltern, Sergeant or any other Corporal took out a patrol and that meant it was only my men that went through the mind shattering experiences. In the very last stage of our war, my section mutinied because of the unrelenting pressure but I will deal with that later.

While we were still in the factory and on just two nights we were given a rum issue. It was supposed to be a warmer before we went on sentry duty, but obviously nobody was going to hang around all night doling out the rum as required and so we had the rum at seven in the evening. Any effect it had was soon dissipated after several hours sleep, and then being woken about three in the morning. We also wondered why we only had the rum twice but were given the answer to that as well. Towards the end of January, the Colour Sergeant and the Old Soldier were discovered to be bedded down in the three ton truck in a glorious and very noisy state of inebriation. The whole Company's rum issue had been put to some good use, and not for the first time we heard. The Colour Sergeant was busted down to Sergeant and the Old Soldier was sent home having just completed his three months tour of duty. The ex Colour Sergeant was posted elsewhere in the battalion and one of our Platoon Sergeants promoted in his place.

From that time on our food and clothing issues were much improved and in spite of lack of attention by those who were supposed to be in charge of our welfare.

CHAPTER EIGHTEEN

The Snow Lay Crisp and Even

It was a particular feature of the campaign that very few enquiries were made by the officers about our living conditions or morale. In Lt. Plum's case it was hardly necessary as we were living cheek by jowl but, in any case, he was not that sort of officer. One particular feature about the snow is that it stayed dry as it were. It was so cold that the snow never thawed out in January or the early part of February, and that was a blessing, believe me. Our feet, socks and boots stayed frozen but without the discomfort of sloshing around in very cold water and slush.

While still in the factory, we heard that the Australians had taken to the habit of drinking anti-freeze as a substitute to alcohol and this had resulted in several going mad and blind, and at least one dying. Nothing was said officially, but I rather feel there was considerable substance to the rumour. Altogether we were fairly light hearted during our stay in the factory and this was due to regular food and regular sleep, and the sheer pleasure of staying in one spot for a long time. Sentry duty was still enforced but we organised so that six men, in pairs, were the sentries for the thirteen hours of darkness. As usual, we only got up once during the night, and that meant the tour of duty was four hours and twenty minutes for each pair. Being so cold though, we had to mark time in the trench for the whole time.

Standing still would have meant freezing to death. At one time my section organised a brazier in the trench but Private Shamrock threw it out one night when in a temper. Perhaps he was thinking of the delights of Seoul.

I don't know when they were issued, but we now had winter sleeping bags. These were two layers of material filled in between with some sort of downy substance. They were deliciously warm and it required an effort to leave such comfort. Lucky were those who spent thirteen hours in sheer bliss.

During the whole time we were in the factory, there was no contact with the other two platoons whatsoever, and I have simply no idea where they were settled down. Whether they were also in some sort of shelter or out in the open remains a mystery. Neither do I remember being at all curious about their condition but in any event it was one constant battle to remain alive at twenty five degrees below zero. Just once in January and for the first and last time during the campaign, we had a visit by a water bowser. We gladly filled up our cans ready for the midday coffee but I was mystified as to how the water was kept from freezing solid. I still don't know the answer to that but perhaps a fire was kept going underneath the truck all night. Obviously the bowser was required at battalion H.Q. as the C.O. and the medical personnel couldn't be running around all the time gathering snow; but I wondered what we would have done without the snow as there were no streams thereabout.

Now is the time to relate the story of my wristwatch. I bought the watch in January 1948 at the then price of nine guineas which was rather unheard of for the working classes. My brother-in-law said, "They saw you coming!" True, the watch was rather small and did not look anything in particular.

Still, I liked it and that was sufficient for me. When we landed in Korea at least one third of the platoon owned a watch, or so it seemed to me. However, when it was realised that we had no guardroom clock to tell us when to change sentries, these watches were extremely important. Both the Platoon Commander and the Platoon Sergeant had watches but steadfastly refused to lend them out. For some mysterious reason all the other watches in the Platoon broke down and then disappeared. It was probably quite true that the watches did founder in the rough conditions as they were mostly of the Mickey Mouse or naked lady type of thing.

Anyway, my watch was the only visible instrument and it was passed on from sentry to sentry all through the night. After a while, I noticed the glass becoming very opaque. It was constantly being burnt by cigarette stubs being held close to the glass in order to ascertain the time. About early January 1951 it was returned to me without any glass at all. I made a substitute by using the plastic spoon from the 'C' rations. I broke off the bowl and bored four holes in each corner. I tied the bowl across the watch and this sufficed. I had to change the cover about every few days but the watch itself never faltered. Now and then a spot of rain or snow got in and lay on the watch face and then rusted. I was able to get a new glass in Tokyo in February but the rust marks remained. It was another thirty eight years before that watch finally retired. I have it still and it is a fond momento! It proved to be well worth the nine guineas. Incidentally, when I returned home in late 1952 I showed the watch to my brother-in-law and told him the history of the last two years. For once he was silent.

While the snow lasted, our frozen water bottles were of no importance whatsoever, but one chap thought he would get his thawed out. He left it fairly near the section fire but standing upright. Of course, it ruptured down the seam, leaving the cork still frozen solid. It was a lesson to us all and we let nature take its course as and when it felt like it, and that wasn't for another two months.

Although we spent long periods just sitting round the fire, we never felt bored but always found something of interest to liven up the conversation. At this stage the enemy was the last thing on our minds. I did wonder at times why we were never used on operations in January but over the years I have realised the truth. With our lack of proper clothing and no facilities for Arctic warfare we simply could not function as a combat unit. The generals had simply put us to one side until the weather got a little less cold.

There was one very interesting development that took place in this month and that was leave to Japan. The first to go on R and R (Rest and Relaxation) was our Platoon Commander Lt. Plum. He was away for about nine days but, on his return, never discussed the event with anyone with the possible exception of the Platoon Sergeant. Two days later, Sgt. Swede took his turn for leave and was also away for nine days. From him we discovered that it took a day to get to the airfield, and the first night was spent in a transit camp. The lucky ones were flown to Tokyo and put up in a large hotel which had been converted into a leave camp. The five days R and R started on the following morning, and then two more days in getting back to the regiment. We had no more details about what happened on the five days leave, but we made some wild guesses! Never though was there any suggestion that R and R would apply to anybody below the rank of Sergeant and that remained so until

I went on leave in February under rather peculiar circumstances.

Whilst Sgt. Swede was away, I was appointed Acting, but unpaid, Platoon Sergeant. My duties were almost non-existent as we were still very static in the factory. I had to collect the 'C' rations in the morning and give those out, and I also had to call the roll in case of any desertions. The British Army in general and the regiment in Korea was paranoid about possible desertions, but in reality there was little to fear. Over the centuries deserters tended to come in three categories. One was those who ran from danger but usually these were easily caught and returned. Two were those who grew bored and sought the fleshpots of the cities or even the delights held by one female in a lonely cottage. Three were those who had no sense of loyalty to a regiment or comrades and were determined to work on the "I'm alright, Jack!" principle. This last category usually had it all worked out and knew where they were headed. In some cases it was into the arms of the enemy!

One of my own men did desert under category three in February 1951 but again this is a story for later on and an explanation of how he got away scot-free.

Otherwise, desertion was out of the question for the regiment. We didn't know where to go if we did desert. We were in a foreign country of which we knew nothing and going over to the enemy was quite out of the question. We knew less about them than we did of the country. In any event, the stigma of cowardice was a very powerful incentive to us all to stay put under any circumstances.

One of my other duties was the collection of replacement shirts, socks and underwear. I had noticed that Sgt. Swede usually returned with one item for each man in the Platoon. We got either a shirt, a pair of socks or a woollen vest or underpants. Thankfully, we did not have to hand in our old item like we did in barracks. These were just thrown away. I can see now the look on the faces of the old Quartermasters when they read this!

Anyway, I got the call to collect the replacement items. Excluding the Platoon Commander, I found we had twenty five men, and so I reasoned I could collect five shirts, five vests, five underpants and ten pairs of socks. I duly presented myself to the Colour Sergeant with my list. I felt quite pleased that there was no argument about my requirements and was walking away when I came under a load of abuse from the other Platoon Sergeants. "Is that all you could get?" they sneered. I was mortified but hurried away. Later, I found out that if I had asked for three times the amount of clothing, it would have been handed over.

Even so, I still never doubted the integrity of Sgt. Swede. There were other incidents later which showed that Sgt. Swede was not the most outstanding NCO of the period but at the time he appeared to be one hellava good chap. It was years before I began to have doubts but by then it didn't matter anyway.

We had one visit by the N.A.A.F.I. wagon while we were still at the factory but very little was bought by the Platoon. The American 'C' rations gave us our daily needs and we all had soap and shaving soap and razor blades and toilet paper and writing pads. I bought some chocolate but all our purchases were made with the thought of "How much more can I carry?" This visit did not stop us grumbling about the rarity of opportunities of buying when we wanted. Back home the N.A.A.F.I. was always there and we rather expected equal facilities in war. Deep down though we knew how difficult it was to bring any vehicle so near the front. The N.A.A.F.I. personnel by the way were all men. None of the weaker sex were allowed anywhere near Korea in the early stages.

After the return of Sgt. Swede we got the order to move elsewhere. It was just after breakfast about 30th January 1951. We only had a few minutes notice but not one of us had abandoned the ingrained habit of having our equipment laid out ready to put on. I had some still wet underwear I was trying to dry, but this simply rolled up in the groundsheet along with blanket and lightweight sleeping bag. I for one had two shocks when I put on my equipment. I had a lump on the top of each shoulder going from the neck to the upper arm. They were muscles developed from the continual carriage of extreme weight. These lumps disappeared within a couple of days along with another lump on my stomach. When I tried to do up my belt I found it impossible. We were already marching along the road and I had to let out the belt a couple of notches either side in order to fasten the buckle. Obviously, in spite of the cold, we enjoyed a fairly easy time for a month. It took two days of hard slog to restore the belt to its original setting, but it was something of an eye opener and a foretaste of my physical shape in years to come.

CHAPTER NINETEEN

The Holiday Is Over

When we got the order to move from the factory, as usual, we had no idea of where we were going and how long it would take. This sort of information was never passed down to the troops, not even at the very end of our tour. I only know I made one bad mistake on that first day. During that first couple of months we had the habit of keeping hold of any likely bits and pieces that might come in handy. As a consequence our load became increasingly heavy. Seeking to make things easier for myself, I threw away the Chinese water bottle, even though mine was still frozen up, and the North Korean Army boots. I was in need of both items in the following days but, even more so, I needed to carry less.

In case any reader is wondering why I spend so much time in writing about these little details, it is because that is the way we lived. Our existence revolved around these very tiny details. There were no parades to get ready for and no inspections by the generals. No marches through the town, no training courses, and absolutely no entertainment of any sort. Even the war was of second rate importance compared to the vital issue of keeping our feet dry.

Soon after we commenced once more to march from one place to another without apparently rhyme or reason, we had a weeks stay in the one place. We were billeted in another deserted village and our daily task was to march to another area to dig a series of slit trenches. This was a fall back position in case of a sudden retreat. None of us had the slightest idea where we were and even less of the position of the enemy. For my part though, this particular week had a different routine from my comrades. From the very first morning I was inflicted with a very painful illness. It started in the small of the back and, during the course of the day, the pain spread upwards to my shoulders and down to my thighs. I was as stiff as a board. I marched to the site of the digging but never actually lifted a spade or pickaxe. I found a hollow and crouched down out of the wind and covered myself over with a groundsheet. I can't remember what I did for a mid day meal but didn't care anyway.

It was established that digging ceased at four o'clock in the afternoon and the platoon marched back to the village for the evening meal. On the first day I was left trailing along far to the rear. On the next four days I used to leave the site at three o'clock, but even so I was always overtaken by the platoon about half way along. When I eventually arrived at the village my meal was waiting ready. When that was over I made ready for bed. I could do very little for myself and I got down on the cottage floor by facing forward while two of my mates held either arm and lowered me down backwards. During the course of the night the pain disappeared completely, leaving me feeling marvellous. Within minutes of standing up the pain started up again and spread all over. During all this time I had not one enquiry about my health from either the Platoon Commander or the Sergeant.

On the sixth day of this procedure, I insisted to myself that I must report sick. To go sick has always been viewed with the utmost suspicion in the British Army and for obvious reasons – and, of course, I immediately felt much better anyway. I went to see the Medical Officer who was suspicious to say the least. He advised that what I had was a bit worse than a very bad cold. He dispensed nine different types of pills. The blue ones twice a day. The pink ones to be taken after meals. The green ones at dawn and dusk and so on and so on. I kept religiously to the set instructions but, in any event, my circumstances changed dramatically. On the morning after we moved off yet again and, like it or lump it, I had to recover, which I did.

In October 1952 I was back home on leave from the Far East and was interested in one particular item of news in the papers. An M.P. (Labour) had been visiting the troops in Korea and had been stricken down with a very painful illness. There was a picture of the M.P. being taken off the plane on a stretcher. The name of the disease was given but I have forgotten this. However, the description of the illness tallied exactly with my attack. There are two points which have intrigued me ever since. Considering the different life styles of the M.P. and myself, what common condition gave us this disease. Secondly, why was no other soldier stricken down? Perhaps a reader may give me the answer.

The next few days were of the same old routine of going up a high ridge, staying the night and coming down again and moving on. The same old practise continued of never informing the common soldier of where he was headed and for why. I must add though that we all remained fairly cheerful in spite of the appalling conditions in which we lived.

Then one day we were part of a huge convoy going from east to west. There were about a hundred vehicles consisting of tanks, jeeps, trucks and many other assorted vehicles. Being so large, the convoy moved very slowly. My platoon occupied one truck of the U.S. Army and driven by a white corporal. Suddenly the truck veered left off the road with the left front wheel embedded in a ditch. Had the ditch not been there, we would have gone down the side of a very steep hill. Being on the inside of the truck and making a lot of noise, we had not heard anything untoward but apparently there had been some firing. We were ordered out and lined the side of the road on the right. The whole convoy had come to a stop, but it was only our driver that had deemed it necessary to take evasive action.

While we were standing around, our driver took the most extraordinary steps ever known on active service. He removed the cap of the petrol filler and then threw lighted matches towards the opening. He explained that he had instructions not to let his vehicle fall into enemy hands. While this was extremely unlikely, it had to be explained to him that we were all in danger of being burnt to a crisp. The poor man was in a complete funk, of course, but for a while about twenty five men were in extreme likelihood of meeting our maker under very distressing circumstances. Twice in a matter of two minutes that driver had very nearly reduced the strength of the British Army by twenty five bodies. I wondered what ever happened to him.

Now, however, we were about to find out where the firing had come from. Where we had halted, the road was lined with a thin belt of trees. 'A' Company had already gone through the trees to start taking up positions in the field beyond. They had come under fire and a Corporal had suffered a severe head wound to his right temple. His brains were hanging out and he had been given up for dead. Then it became evident that he was still alive and was carried out of danger. The whole of 'A' Company also left the field, but I have no idea where they went. My platoon was then ordered into the same field but before we could do much we also came under fire, but I appeared to be the only one to realise the situation. In line with the road, and about one hundred yards away, was a line of bushes and from the base there came a series of flashes. I was only barely aware of bullets going past, but nobody else appeared to have noticed.

I yelled to my section to take cover and return fire. They got down and took up position, but the rise of the ground prevented them from even seeing the bushes. The Platoon Commander and the Sergeant were just looking on in amazement. I took up my Sten gun and fired a few bursts at the base of the bushes. The flashes ceased immediately and never resumed. About fifteen minutes later we got the order to resume our onward movement. Our company did this on foot as our intended positions were only a mile away.

Having settled down for the day, a couple of subalterns came round with the story that the mystery firers were a group of South Korean troops who had mistaken us for the Chinese. Even then this fable was simply unbelievable. There was no evidence at that time that the Chinese had any trucks so far forward, never mind tanks and all covered with American divisional signs, and remember the South Korean Army was entirely equipped from American sources. We all wore the same uniform. We could just believe that the firers were South Koreans, but the story fell apart on one sound basis. Having opened fire in the first instance, no Korean soldier, North or South, would have stayed in position. They would simply have run away very fast. After all, they were faced with scores of trucks and tanks and thousands of armed men. For my part, I believe the firers were Chinese, and they would have stayed where they were until it was made obvious that they had nothing more to gain.

Still more amazing was the fact that thousands of troops just sat there awaiting orders – orders that never came in spite of hundreds of senior officers who were on hand to take the initiative. To my mind, the fable of the South Korean ambushers was put about to explain the lack of action by the senior officers. As an afterthought of this particular incident, I must explain what happened to the wounded Corporal. His physical wound was patched up in Japan, but he was left with brain damage. In about June 1951 in Hong Kong I overheard a conversation between some of our wounded who had now rejoined the regiment. Apparently the Corporal would be listening to conversations and joking but would laugh about two minutes after everyone else. He was incapable of making any sense with his words but there he was, still in Japan. He was wounded in February and this was now June and there was no suggestion that he would be returned to the U.K. This happened to all our wounded. They simply stayed in Japan and in dire contrast to the U.S. troops who were all sent "Stateside" as soon as possible.

This peculiar happening, like many others, was never mentioned in the book "The Diehards in Korea". Probably out of sheer embarrassment!

About this time we were made aware that we had a new Company Commander. He was a cheerful sounding chap but was rather old for someone who had to survive in these very arduous conditions. I wasn't aware, of course, of the insider fighting that went on between the Regular Army Officers of those days in competing for a chance to command on active service. The road from Sandhurst to General Command was strewn with the bodies of those who never quite made it. Promotion to the rank of Major was certain but, thereafter, it was by selection. A couple of Campaign medals for wars other than World War Two were highly prized as an aid to promotion. Perhaps our new Major thought he still had a chance as he was selected for service in Korea on seniority. His fate was decided within a month.

Our daily wanderings continued and were only made notable by the height of the hills we climbed. One day we had a climb that beat all the others into a cocked hat. Two companies set off on a path that led upwards. We went up and up and up. Each section and platoon were at first in strict order, but within an hour men began to drop out for a rest. Sometimes we had to haul ourselves onward on our hands and knees. Sometimes forcing our bodies through thick brambles, but always upward. After two hours there was no particular order of march. The platoons were all mixed up. I insisted that each member of my section take a turn in carrying the Bren gun but I took my turn last and this meant I carried it for the last two hours of our five hour hike. The climb really was a stupendous achievement and I can only suppose it was all worth it for tactical reasons.

On reaching the top, which was a ridge stretching along for about two hundred yards, I saw Lt. Plum. He seemed remarkably composed and was holding what appeared to be a map. He had obviously already received instructions about our fire positions, but from where I could not say. I was dimly aware that someone was in charge but for the life of me I can't remember Company Headquarters being up on that ridge.

Obviously my memory is at fault. Lt. Plum told me, "Your section will be along here!" I slumped to the ground and did not move for another fifteen minutes. All during the campaign I had taken some pride in the fact that I was always first up a hill, no matter what. I was now somewhat downhearted in the knowledge that I was not the first by a long chalk, and I had even been overtaken by many others. It was some climb though.

CHAPTER TWENTY

The Only Enemy Was Ourselves

In spite of the exhausting climb we still had to go through the motions of expecting the enemy to be close at hand and ready to charge into our positions without warning. I suppose it made sense, but I looked towards the direction of the Chinese Forces and saw the hill was just as steep on their side and covered with scrub and forest. A silent approach was impossible unless they took a week to climb the hill. Nonetheless, sentries were placed at all times.

Before we started that climb the Battalion had received some reinforcements from the Royal Fusiliers. As they had to be aged nineteen to come to Korea, they must have been with the Royal Fusiliers in Germany before I left them in June 1950 but I don't remember them. Almost certainly they were with another Company. It never crossed my mind to ask them though. Later on I was to come across a Lieutenant and a Corporal from my old Company but they had been placed elsewhere in the Regiment.

Anyway, I had two National Servicemen posted to my section but I had not the time to even question them about their state of military training. One was a nondescript sort of chap and would have fitted in anywhere. However, he was completely under the spell of his companion. This other chap was beefy in build and with a loud mouth. For some reason he felt compelled to challenge all and sundry to a fist fight in order to establish his personal bravery. It all washed over the rest of us but his companion went in utter awe of him.

That night I placed the two of them together on sentry duty. A bad mistake! At about midnight a shot rang out and two companies of troops went instantly to their trenches. (A Company was with us up this hill). I knew straight away that it was my sentries that had fired and I plonked myself down beside them. "Where are they?" I asked. "I thought I saw something!" Big Mouth replied. My mind reeled. Never had it been known in the Company for anyone to fire on sentry duty on the off chance there might be something out there. I could see my stripes being ripped off my arm by the Regimental Sergeant Major. I could only mutter, "Don't do it again!" I went off to report to the Platoon Commander and he reported to the Company Commander and so on. I felt so humiliated. "It was my sentry". The Companies settled down again but I never heard another word.

Big Mouth though had shown himself for what he really was. A piece of jelly when it really mattered. For the rest of the Campaign he was fairly subdued but back in Hong Kong he was all mouth once more and always looking for a fight with chaps smaller than himself.

But before that, we had to get on and dig our slit trenches and sort out our sleeping places. There was one big worry though. We had no water at all. Our water bottles had been emptied on the way up. Then came a shout. "I've found some water!" One of the chaps in the Company had come across a spring and we were almost at the top of this very high hill. It was only a trickle of water though and it took ages to find a spot on the granite from which we could fill a bottle. Then I spotted that the water fell into a natural bowl in the rock. This bowl was the size of a kitchen sink, but it was full to the brim with dead leaves and other disgusting matter deposited by the small deer and other animal life.

I got to though and scraped out an immense amount of filth and what have you. There were several gallons of water swirling around in the bowl but it was a dark brown colour. I went away and returned in half an hour. I was extremely satisfied with my efforts. The bowl was full of clear sparkling champagne. I notified all of our Company and 'A' Company as well. Of course, we never drank the water as it was but boiled it up for the brews of cocoa and coffee in our 'C' rations. As it happened, water was brought up the hill by the Colour Sergeant and his team of Korean porters. What a magnificent job those porters did.

I thought at the time we had no more worries about the water but I was wrong. A couple of hours later, I went to fill up the section brew can but noticed that there was a white scum all round the rim of the rock bowl. I looked closely and smelt the scum and it came to me. Some selfish bastard had actually washed and shaved directly into that pure water. How anyone could have been so self centred I just don't know. I dipped the can into the centre of the bowl and took it back to boil up. The result was to be a drink of soapy tasting coffee and then soapy tasting cocoa. I hope the culprit is reading this and has the decency to apologise.

After climbing up that hill we descended again the following day. The effort wasn't quite as bad but bad enough. In front of me was a chap I hadn't seen before. I think he was from 'A' Company. Anyway he started up a monologue of complaints about everyone and everything. I suppose it was his way of getting through the ordeal. After half an hour I told him to shut up. He looked at me in total surprise and was obviously very hurt. I didn't care. I wasn't going to go through that for a couple of hours.

CHAPTER TWENTY ONE

The Real Thing

By the 13th February 1951 we still had not seen hide nor hair of the enemy, but there were ample reports coming in from various sources. Incidentally, when I say enemy, it is always the Chinese. If the North Korean Army was still in action it was never in any sector where we were engaged. On the 13th we went up yet another ridge and came under fire for the first time in two months. It was medium machine gun fire from the Australians. They had been ordered to give us covering fire but some of the rounds were falling short. By the Grace of God nobody was hit. Once again, we did not see the enemy and we came down off that ridge with some relief.

The next day saw the battalion committed to capturing a hill from the Chinese. This hill came to be called Hill 181 and it was rather like a pork chop sitting in the middle of a very large baking dish. All around the hill was flat ground with no cover and the only road ran along the left hand side of the valley.

We already had reports that the Chinese had ambushed an entire U.S. Regimental Combat Team and inflicted enormous casualties. These reports turned out to be only too true. An R.C.T. is equivalent to one of the British Infantry Brigades. In essence, about three thousand fighting troops. The engagement had happened a mile or so up the road from Hill 181 and the enemy were now in occupation of the ridge. My regiment had been ordered to take Hill 181 from the enemy. The advance was led by one of the other companies and the first man to attempt the climb was a Sergeant who had been called up from the reserve.

One of our reinforcement contingents was made up of men who had been released from the Army on expiration of a regular engagement, i.e. seven years with the Colours and five years on the reserve. Sometimes this was five and seven and even three and nine. Come the end of World War Two and these terms of service caused a great deal of confusion. Before the War really got under way, hundreds of thousands of young men flocked to join the services but found, as yet, that they couldn't join for the duration of emergency. They joined up as regulars anyway and were confident they would be released when hostilities were over. Many a Recruiting Sergeant must have had curses heaped upon them in 1945 and 1946.

In fact, hundreds if not thousands were discharged according to their Age and Service Number when the War ended and then found they were recalled to complete their service as a Regular. The Age and Service Number was allocated to everybody in the Services and indicated when they were likely to be discharged. My number was sixty six and this group were released in January 1947.

Apart from the heartaches suffered in 1945 there came an additional complication in 1950 on the outbreak of War in Korea. All the reservists were recalled to the Colours to complete their twelve years and, in addition, were committed to serve for at least eighteen months regardless of when their reserve service expired. For instance, a chap signing on for seven and five in September 1939 was committed to serve in any capacity until September 1951. If he was recalled in Jan. 1951 his service actually expired in July 1952.

There was one famous case of a man who signed on with the Royal Sussex Regiment in about Nov. 1938. He served in the Desert but was taken prisoner in 1942. On release he discharged to the reserve but was recalled to the Colours in Sept. 1950. The day his twelve years expired he was photographed walking up the gangplank of the troopship taking him to Korea. This man, on arrival in Korea, was allocated to my Company but was not around for very long. I think some cushy number was found for him in the rear area. Forty years later, a British woman tourist in New York found his medals in a pawn shop. She brought them back to this country and there was a bit of a story in the papers but the man himself was never traced. If still alive in 2000 he would be at least eighty three but probably nearer ninety.

Just before the incident of Hill 181 I was given a L/Cpl as my Second-in-Command. He was one of those who had rushed to sign up for five and seven in 1939 but had joined the Royal Corps of Signals where he served as a driver for the whole of the War. He had no experience at all of infantry soldiering and none as a Leader. He was now twenty nine years of age, married with two small children and was a Boy Scout Commander. He took a lot of ribbing about that but took it all in good part. Try as he might, he could not influence my section into doing anything they objected to. A thoroughly nice man, but a fish out of water. He came over in the same batch as the Sergeant I mentioned earlier.

But to get back to the assault on Hill 181. The Sergeant led the way as I have said, but was stopped in his tracks by a bullet between the eyes. His death caused a hold up for a while but when the Company started up the ridge again it was to find the Chinese had fled. The whole of the ridge was occupied by three Companies with one in reserve together with Battalion Headquarters. My Company was third in line and we occupied the long stem of the pork chop with two other Companies forward on the knuckle.

Before we set off though I was sent with my section to reconnoitre the ground around the left of the hill. There was no more small arms fire or shelling by the Canadians but I was going into unknown country. The first item we came across was a dead U.S. soldier. He was a black man and he was lying back on a steep slope, almost upright, and his arms were stretched above his head. There was a bullet hole in his right arm pit and I surmise he was shot in the act of surrender. His weapon was gone as was the ammunition.

The next item of interest was a dead Chinaman. Everything about him looked intact and he was huge for an Oriental. The only trace of damage was a small tear at his right knee with some bloodstains. A shell had come from behind and exploded at his feet. He had not been dead for very long and his companions must have retreated only minutes before. The dead man was holding an American carbine and this I took for myself along with some magazines of ammo. I finished the recce and rejoined the Platoon. I was highly delighted with my trophy as the Sten gun I had carried all this time was very inappropriate for hill warfare. Or at least, I thought so.

I now had a shock. The other two Section Commanders had both been shot through the left arm. They were both Irishmen and very inferior Section Leaders. I distrusted them as any type of soldier. I instantly surmised that they had got down in a hole somewhere, faced each other with weapons cocked and at an agreed signal shot each other. Many years later, Lt. Plum told me over the phone that he blamed the Second-in-Command of the Company for sending him forward towards the enemy. I have never had a proper explanation for that incident and it remains a mystery to me.

We now had to start digging in once more but before doing so, I went down the hill and found the Company truck. I deposited my Sten gun and magazines in the back and returned to the section quite happy. While I was away, Lt. Plum had decided where the usual slit trenches had to be dug. While we were preparing for this activity one of my chaps shouted out, "That went straight past my ear!" Some of the other Companies were firing their Bren guns at an enemy position about five hundred yards away and across the road. I presumed my chap had a vivid imagination. It was me that was wrong, as later other bullets arrived in our area.

My Platoon was sited on a path that ran right along the ridge from the knuckle to the end of the chop. On the forward slope, i.e. completely without any cover, Lt. Plum had placed one of the sections without a Leader. They had a Lance Corporal but for the moment he was just one of the chaps. The other two sections plus Platoon Headquarters were placed behind the ridge with ample cover and with two other Platoons between us and the valley floor. From the forward slope, because of a bulge in the ground, nobody could see further than twenty yards. A rush by the Chinese could have over ran the lonely section in seconds.

After a while, that section began to panic as the odd shot was fired in our direction. The men began to shout, "We're not stopping here!" Neither Lt. Plum or Sgt. Swede left their position of safety although the anguished shouts could clearly be heard. There was nothing for it. I simply had to do something. I strolled down to that section with my hands in my pockets. I pretended there was no danger but my heart was beating very fast. The young lads looked up at me with awe but the trick worked. They stayed where they were but my contempt for Lt. Plum was beginning to grow. By this time he had developed a little trick of his own. When things got rough he would take out a map and study it closely. He would gaze all around as though he was working out possible lines of fire and other military matters. He would be lying down, of course. When the firing died down he would put the map away but he still never left his position of safety. Not a single word of encouragement was ever known to pass his lips.

Sgt. Swede was nearly as bad but at least he gave me an explanation many years later. "I tried to help him and would tell him to go forward and see to such and such a section. He would reply, 'There's no need. They will be all right!'"

As a consequence Sgt. Swede would also stay where he was out of sheer loyalty but he later made amends.

It was the afternoon now and we then saw one of the ironic tragedies of warfare. A sergeant of the U.S. Army was crawling along the road from the direction of the enemy. He had been shot through both legs and, as we heard later, had been crawling along that road all night. Anyway, wireless contact had been made with Rear H.Q. and a Land Rover was sent forward to pick up the Sergeant. They were only about two hundred yards from the enemy but no shots were fired.

CHAPTER TWENTY TWO

The Big Attack

Once we had got settled down in our positions, we sorted out our sleeping spaces and then began to dig our slit trenches. Quite surprisingly the soil was quite soft and we were able to dig a trench that was waist high when occupied. Come nightfall and we were in a fair position of defence. Eating a meal was, of course, a matter of high priority but for the life of me I just can't remember fifty years later having a meal on Hill 181. Did the Company supply us with a meal or did we have 'C' rations. I can't believe that the exciting events that followed could drive out the memory of food. In any event, there was no fuel on Hill 181 so we must have been supplied by the Company cooks.

Anyway, it was now dark and we were preparing to get down to sleep. We had prepared our sleeping space and put up our pup tents. These two man tents supplied by the United States were an absolute Godsend. But now came Lt. Plum who had been called to a conference with the other officers of three Companies. A patrol had to be sent out and, as usual, I was to be the leader. In three rifle Companies there are nine subalterns, nine sergeants and twenty seven section leaders but, once again, I was chosen to lead the patrol. At the time, I had a sneaking feeling that Lt. Plum had been designated to lead the patrol but had chosen instead to nominate me.

But first came some terrible confusion. Lt. Plum was giving me some instructions and pointed to a portion of the ridge we were occupying and said, "You will go up that hill and have a look round." I was shocked out of my skull. He was pointing to the higher end of the pork chop. In reality, the knuckle end of the pork chop was two small hills connected by a short ridge. From the top of one hill, the highest one, to the top of the other was no more than eighty yards. I just could not believe that we had not occupied both hills when we had driven off the enemy from the whole of the pork chop.

I asked and pointed, "Did you say **that** hill?"

"Yes," he replied in exasperation. I remained silent but resolved to go very carefully. When the time came, I led my section down a ravine until we were at the base of the appointed hill. My tactical lessons learned at the School of Infantry screamed out that our troops **must** have occupied that hill. Just then we heard a noise. It was someone coming down the ridge. I challenged the person with the daily password and got the correct reply in English. He turned out to be the Company Sergeant Major of 'A' Company. He asked what we were doing and I told him we were on a patrol to have a look around over there and I pointed across the valley. We struck out for the far side and left the CSM to carry on with his toilet arrangements. He was carrying a shovel, but nothing else. He was also very lucky that night. I silently cursed Lt. Plum for his inefficiency.

I led the patrol across the valley and to the ridge on the right hand side. I worked out that this was the supposed hill, but it was a ridge that led from one end of the valley to the other. I could see in the semi-dark that it was perfect for a large party of the enemy to lie in wait to ambush any patrols. The smooth hillside went upwards and over the brow and we could see no further than ten yards at any time. I led the way up and my heart was pumping away ten to the gallon. We were almost at the top when Private Shamrock said, "Let's go!" and went down the hill. The rest followed in a hurry and so did I. I reported that the ridge was unoccupied and by sheer luck events showed that I told the truth. Mind you, the Chinese **should** have been on that ridge but their tactics were at fault and perhaps their courage as well. In addition, they did not have unlimited manpower as we discovered the next day.

Getting down to sleep for the rest of the night was no problem but there was one snag. The snow over which we marched in the February sun was beginning to melt and, as a consequence, our boots were now wet. I for one pulled open the laces and widened the uppers as far as possible. I reasoned that it was going to take some minutes to put them on in the morning, but I couldn't keep them on all night. The weather was still well below freezing. Neither did I make any suggestions to my section. We had all learnt by this time that it was best to sort these things out for ourselves, then no one could be blamed. I think my tent partner kept his boots on, but that was courting disaster from frostbite. However, it turned out for the best.

At about five o'clock in the morning, all hell broke loose. There was yelling and firing all around the two forward Companies. We were fully dressed except for boots, and were lying on one groundsheet and a blanket with another groundsheet and blanket on top, In addition, we were inside a summer sleeping bag and all inside the pup tent. My first reaction was to reach for the catch on the zip fastener of the sleeping bag. My breath had frozen and the zip was stuck. I was in a panic but managed to get the zip moving downwards. I struggled out and picking up my boots in one hand and carrying my carbine in the other, I ran across the ice in my stockinged feet. I jumped down into the slit trench but stubbed one set of toes on the far side of the trench. I didn't feel any pain. I just knew what I had done. I managed to slip on my boots but there was no question of doing up the laces. Just then I heard several cries for help from the other men of my Platoon. I ran back to assist them in undoing the zips. It was quite a job. Back to the trench again, and I made sure all my men were there. I also checked on the men of the forward section who were still in a panic. Except for the odd shot from across the valley, my Company was not actually engaged in the battle.

My Platoon Commander had jumped into his trench and stayed there. I was concerned with my men and also with the other section. In order to be seen by both sections, I sat on the path that led along the ridge and stayed there all night, completely in the open. It was all I could do to stop the men deserting their posts. All the while the battle raged nobody from Company Headquarters paid a visit to the Platoons. This seemed to be the way of life with my Company. Once the shooting started, the Platoons were left to their own devices. There was a reasonable excuse when the Company was spread over some very high ground, but Hill 181 was a comparatively shallow area. All the same, nobody came to have a look see.

While the battle was still raging among the forward Companies, I saw two figures stumbling towards me. I stopped them and saw it was two very young soldiers who were gibbering with fright and I could not blame them. One had a slight wound on the neck and the other was leading him to the Aid Post. Obviously a very composed officer had detailed the unwounded one to get his comrade to the rear. A very wise move, as both were utterly useless as soldiers in that condition. While I was speaking to these two, I was practically standing on my Platoon Commander's hands but he never even looked up. Neither did the Sergeant.

The battle subsided and we waited for the dawn. Later, we had reports that nine of the Die-hards had died in battle and about twenty were wounded. The Roll of Honour shows that seven died on the 15th February but that roll shows the day they died rather than when they were hit.

Later reports showed that some of the dead were bayoneted while still in their sleeping bags, and this I can believe when I think of my own difficulty with the zip. The Forward Observation Officer from the New Zealand Artillery had operated his wireless set with one hand while firing his Sten gun with the other. He was awarded the Military Cross. Incidentally, the New Zealand 25 Pounder Regiment always responded magnificently when their services were required. The two forward Companies were already at stand to when the attack was launched and this foresight undoubtedly saved the day. But it also contradicts the report of men dying in their sleeping bags. Certainly my Company had only normal sentries out and so I can't explain the confusion.

The "Die-hards in Korea" has just one sentence for the action on the 16th of February. This reads as follows:- "In the morning, 'C' Company went forward to collect up the enemy wounded." I will now write on the 16th of February as I experienced it...

In the middle of the morning, the whole Company was assembled in two or three lines, going from the base of our hill to the ridge which I had not properly explored. We then advanced in three lines towards the enemy position. My Platoon was leading. The enemy, dead and wounded, were lying all over the ground in front of the forward Company positions, but to one side there were a group of about fifteen all bunched together. As we started turning over the bodies one of the Chinese suddenly sat up all smiles. He pulled up one trouser leg and showed a tiny shrapnel wound near his shin. We ignored him and carried on with the search. I did notice though one chap lying face down and sort of snorting. I wondered why these two were still alive. It was well below freezing point, and they had been there for hours. None of the other bodies showed signs of life, and I thought they had all been wounded and gathered together to be picked up later.

Perhaps though I was wrong again as I noticed that every single one of the enemy was equipped with two American arms. Either two rifles or two carbines or one of each. They also wore U.S. Army overshoes and carried American shell dressings. I never noticed any Chinese or Korean weapons among them. There was no doubt that they were part of the raiding party that had wiped out the American R.C.T. but I cannot explain why this party had all been hit in the one place and so close together.

We carried on with the search, but I did notice, with relief, that the enemy had advanced from the end of the valley a distance of about three hundred yards. Had they lay hidden on the ridge, they would have only had to travel about fifty yards. A run like that would have meant the battalion would have been in dire danger. I still thank my lucky stars when I think of that close run thing.

We went onto the end of the valley. Here was a small copse of trees. A man made copse as all the trees and bushes had been planted deliberately in order to reclaim some of the land from the ever hungry peasants who needed the soil for rice growing. Before entering the copse, however, we needed to step up onto a flat area which was as long as the copse and about fifteen yards wide. This flat area was about eighteen inches higher than the surrounding fields and this eighteen inches became very important in a short space of time. Going through the copse, we actually came to the end of the valley. Stretching upwards before us was a grassy slope and seemingly innocent of all danger. Suddenly, there was the proverbial buzzing of bees and hundreds of bullets were being fired at the Platoon. Turning with my back to the hill, I yelled to the Platoon to get back. At the same time, I was dimly aware that an object had come from the copse and landed about six feet from my back. There was an explosion and the blast went all over my body. One of my men shouted, "Eh! There's some gooks in here!" but nobody really took any notice.

In the scramble to get back to the flat area, the gooks were ignored. There were two of them as it happened, and what brave men they were. They had crouched down while we went past and they were in just as much danger from the bullets fired by their comrades as we were. I actually saw the two gooks as I went back but I was too concerned about my section at the time to do anything. Gathering at the edge of the copse and wondering what to do, there came some orders from Company Headquarters to send in a search and find patrol. I and my men were immediately selected by Lt. Plum. I went back to the copse and lay down waiting for things to go quieter. Private Shamrock said, "I've been hit!" and indeed a bullet had gone through four layers of clothing from front to back, but without actually touching the skin. "Never mind!" said Shamrock. "That will do!" It was to be about two weeks before I found out what he meant.

In the meantime, a Bren gun crew had kindly laid down covering fire from the end of the copse and going across our front. As I started edging forward, I received a cheery wave from the Lance Corporal in charge. I continued crawling forward, but the Bren gun crew never stopped firing. I was getting closer and closer to the bullets pinging off the trees, but still they continued firing. I turned to tell someone in my Platoon to get the Bren gun crew to cease, but I could see nobody. Twenty men, including the Lt. and the Sgt. had vanished. Me and my section were all alone with not a hope of support. I gave up in disgust and went back to find the Platoon. I had to go to the far edge of the flat area to find them. They were all lying down along the step with eighteen inches of earth protecting them. Not one had a weapon ready to give covering fire. One man with a sub-machine gun could have wiped out the lot.

I looked down at Lt. Plum with some amazement but he never moved. Indeed, his batman was lying on top of his legs giving him added protection. Lt. Plum never asked how I got on and never suggested any sort of protection for me and my men. The one sided trench was full up and so I told my men to spread themselves on the paddy field. I went and sat down alongside a solitary tree that was growing at the edge. It was half the width of my body but it was something. I was then given an explanation by the Sergeant that the Australians were giving covering fire with their machine guns but some shots were falling short. As the Platoon had their backs to the Australians, I found this excuse rather weak.

I then noticed that indeed we were under fire, but I doubt if anybody else knew about this particular danger. A lone rifleman was firing from our right and he was atop a hill and about three hundred yards distance. His shots were landing in the paddy field in front of me, and within a circle of about six feet across. The firer was at a disadvantage though. He could not see the strike of his shots in the soft earth, and so continued to miss his intended target. I thought of telling Lt. Plum but reasoned that would only make him panic.

Just then another event occurred that would change all our plans. A stretcher party came in view from around the corner of the copse to our left. We were informed by the Platoon nearest that the casualty was our Company Commander. He had simply collapsed amidst all the excitement. This Major had joined us after Capt. Blackberry had gone on to other things in another part of the world. He was a cheerful character and a veteran of World War Two but never, ever made himself known to the Company. We common soldiers only saw him in passing, as it were. Apparently he was high on the list to be made Lt./Col. and needed service in Korea to clinch the deal. That promotion was now dead as a doornail.

CHAPTER TWENTY THREE

From The Shooting To The Shouting

Our day was not done however. There came a new danger. The two Gooks we had left in the copse had crept forward to our side and started throwing grenades. The first one landed about fifteen yards from the Platoon lying in the ditch. The second one about ten yards from the men. The third one about five yards, at which time somebody yelled out, "Heh! That's a grenade!" but nobody moved. I had thrown myself flat on the ground each time, with my head towards the explosion, but with my hands covering my skull. Better to lose a finger, I reasoned, than have a splinter in my brain. I could also have run far, far away, but it just never entered my head. I did, however, suggest to myself that something ought to be done.

I stood up with my carbine at the ready. When I saw the next grenade in the air, I fired two quick shots in the direction of the thrower and flung myself flat and waited for the explosion. From the time the lever is released from the grenade and the fuse starts burning there are four seconds before the grenade goes off. Ample time for my particular action. At my fifth attempt to get the thrower or his mate, I saw a branch being violently shaken. Then it was still. No more grenades came our way. The next day, an abandoned bloodstained rifle was found at the spot, but I was on my way to Japan for some leave. I will come back to that incident later. In the meantime, not another person had moved although they were all in deadly danger. It was the example that was set by the Platoon Commander that paralysed the men. Out of instinctive loyalty to the officer class, I never vented my feelings to anybody.

I sat down again by the tree and watched the dirt spurting up from the fire of the sniper, but otherwise there wasn't a sound from anybody. Then the second-in-command, Capt. Orange, filtered down an order to retreat. Instantly, Lt. Plum leapt to his feet and led the helter skelter back to our position on Hill 181. There wasn't a counting of heads to ensure that all were present. On the way, Lt. Plum blundered into a Corporal who had a bullet through his leg. He wasn't from our Platoon and I don't know when he was hit, but Lt. Plum got him under one arm with a soldier at the other side. They got him back to safety but ever after Lt. Plum gave himself much credit for his gallant action. Never a word though about lying in a ditch for three hours or more without saying a word.

I myself started running with the rest but then I became disgusted at all and sundry for running away from the enemy. We had been shot at by a couple of hundred Chinese. Grenades had been thrown at us and a sniper kept up a fusillade of shots. We on the other hand had done absolutely nothing. My own actions I counted as strictly self defence, which it was. I felt that we should have at least tried an attack on the hill occupied by our foes. On reflection though, I was probably wrong in my attitude. Military tactics in those days required an attacking force to be two hundred strong against an enemy force of one hundred, and across flat ground. Uphill required four hundred together with covering fire from artillery and mortars. At best we were outnumbered by about two to one. Retreat was the correct decision in the circumstances, but I still felt disgusted.

Half way back to safety, I started to walk but in doing so I was left entirely alone. I could feel two hundred rifles trained on my back, but not a shot was fired in my direction. Nothing though was going to make me run any more. As I got in among the forward Company, an officer asked if I was wounded, but I told him no. He looked at me as if I was insane and he was probably right. I felt so disgusted though. During that day we had all suffered considerable small arms fire. My Platoon had a grenade attack as well as sniper fire. A Major had collapsed and a Corporal was wounded. Later that night there was a deserter and about one hundred men had suffered another nail in the coffin of shell-shock. This then was the day described as "In the morning 'C' Company went forward to gather up the enemy wounded." As it so happened, the wounded were attended to by another Company.

Back in our old positions, we just got on with our old routine...doing absolutely nothing unless ordered to do otherwise. We had all learnt to get as much rest as possible as we never knew what was coming next. Then we had another shock. A corporal came down to our position and announced, "I've been sent for to help shoot the prisoners." The corporal was an ex-Public School Boy who had failed to become a commissioned officer. His eyes were shining with delight at the prospect of his task. I was shocked out of my skull with the announcement, but I watched him go off towards the group of dead and wounded we had encountered earlier. In due course we heard a number of shots fired. I turned away and tried to forget all about the incident. It was years before I realised that the shooting party was under the direction of the Regimental

Medical Officer. The group were indeed all wounded men who had been gathered together for recovery later, but that opportunity was denied them by the Battalion who had not retreated under fire as was expected by the enemy.

Even when my Company came across them, the majority were all perfectly still. With the temperature at minus twenty degrees they were slowly freezing to death. By the afternoon they were more than likely dead. The Medical Officer could probably detect only the faintest sign of life in just a few and resuscitation was not an option. Even if some could be brought back to life, they would have no arms or legs or faces. A bullet through the brain was a kindness. Had the circumstances been explained to me, I would most likely have volunteered for the shooting party, but I would not have done it with my eyes shining with glee.

While it was still light I had another shock. The Sergeant asked me if I would like to go on leave to Tokyo. I was delighted at the prospect and agreed. I had a moment of guilt when I realised that I would be leaving my section who were all entitled to leave, but there was no chance of three year regulars and National Servicemen being given a holiday. In my Company at least, no corporal went on R and R until all the Officers and Sergeants had been sent to Japan. Indeed I can't remember if any other Corporal was ever sent from my Company. What I could not understand is how the vacancy came about amidst all that shooting and what not. With years of hindsight, I now realise that I had been chosen not for my exploits during the day but simply to stop me talking. Not that I would have talked anyway. My loyalty was still very strong, if a little dented around the edges. Even now, while writing this,

I have doubts about my loyalty but then again, what's the point of any book of this nature if we don't tell the truth.

I went down the path to where Regimental Headquarters were located and reported to someone about my leave. I was bedded down somewhere for the night and put on a truck for the airport in the morning. Somewhere along the way I left my ammo pouches together with belt and grenades and stuff like that, but kept my small pack with change of underwear. I was also required to keep my carbine. At the airport, we went through various documentation procedures and shown the dining hall and finally the sleeping quarters, which were tents, for the night. Except, in my case, I was shown a place where there were some bedsteads in a sort of shed. I slept there entirely alone. The excuse that was given was that the tents were full up. In reality, the authorities did not like my appearance. My Combat Jacket and Trousers and Boots were covered in grime and grease and mud from five months of continuous wear in all weathers and all conditions. From frequent marches up hill and down dale, my clothing was also heavily impregnated with sweat. I was not a nice person to know but, of course, back in the Company we were all the same and did not notice.

I had to go on the 'plane as I was but I never noticed any particular objection by anyone. As far as I was concerned, we all looked the same but perhaps I was wrong. The passengers were from all the British regiments in Korea together with the Australians. The Australians had better reason than most to look forward to leave. The Royal Australian Regiment were already in Japan when the Korean War started and they were no strangers to the social life. On arrival in Tokyo we were taken to the leave camp, actually a large hotel. First we stripped off all our clothing and, retaining only our Combat Jacket and

Trousers and webbing equipment, went through a shower. We were all asked if we were carrying any "little strangers" with us but all were able to answer, "No!".

After going through the shower, we got dried and were then issued with an entirely new set of clothing: socks, underwear, shirt and battledress. Our heavy duty pullover though we kept for some unknown reason. We had already deposited our weapons in the guardroom and we were shown our quarters. Six of us, all from the Middlesex Regiment, were in the same room. One corporal was much older than the rest of us and we looked to him for guidance as to what to do. It was still early afternoon and five of us ventured out to town. We had been paid in American dollar script and this we had to change in a bank. The exchange rate meant we were issued the appropriate yen right down to the last half farthing. Some of the notes were never used by the Japanese as they were of such small value. They were exquisite works of art and brand new. I kept mine for years until they were "claimed" by my children.

The sixth member of our room, a Corporal Large, never left the camp except to buy a guitar, and on this he practised for five days in isolation. When the Battalion arrived back in Britain, Sergeant Large was seen greeting his fiancée with a guitar strung across his back. I wonder what happened to the three of them! For five of us our first day of R and R was fairly quiet. First of all, I went to a watchmaker to have my watch cleaned up and a glass fitted to take the place of the plastic spoon tied over the face. The watch incidentally had never stopped working even though some flakes of snow had rusted onto the dial. I had the watch returned in perfect order but the rust marks remained. Next I bought a camera with three rolls of film. In Korea I hoarded the film and got to Hong Kong with one and a half rolls intact. I did think about buying a pair of shoes but decided against the idea. They would have been thrown away at the end of five days.

Our first evening was a quiet affair as we were still feeling our way around. A friendly taxi driver steered us to a huge night club which was a favourite of the Yanks. There were literally hundreds of GI's with a seeming obsession to make as much noise as possible. A floor show consisted of the customary stripper who divested herself of clothing until one tiny piece remained. This was removed at the same time as the lights went out and we had to wonder if we had actually seen the "forbidden". The Yanks though screamed louder than ever and some stood on the tables. We British remained stone faced and left after half an hour. I was later to realise that the GI's were losing themselves in drink in order that they had an excuse not to indulge themselves with the hostesses. Later at home they would brag about the girls they laid all night and all day, but it would be lies. Typical boys trying to be men.

Back at the hotel and preparing for an early night, I was aware of a growling sort of noise. I went down the corridor until the noise got louder. I saw a door marked "Bar" and opened it. Inside were about two hundred British squaddies swallowing beer and singing and shouting. They were behaving just like the Yanks. Later, I was able to work out that fully ninety five per cent of those on R and R never left the camp at all, but stayed in the bar. Like the GI's though, the stories told at home became ever more lurid as the years went by.

I will not reveal any more of my exploits in Tokyo except to confess that I lost my virginity – and was I glad of that! No more would I have to pretend when the stories were going around. Not that I ever boasted about something that had never taken place, but was I pleased with myself that I could now remain silent and listen to the others with their boasting. I had done it and that improved my confidence. I thought of the lads back in Korea and wondered what I could take back as presents. The choice was severely limited as it would not do to take back something they would have to carry for evermore. In the end, I settled for British cigarettes and chocolate. Neither was actually needed but they made a change from the U.S./'C' rations.

Before I returned, I was made aware that a Roman Catholic chapel was available for a brief service. I never took advantage of the offer, but it made me think. Only about five times did we have the Roman Catholic Padre of the Brigade perform a service in the field, and I attended as an insurance policy. Over the years I have neglected my faith, but never abandoned it altogether. In recent years, I have been accustomed to attend Mass every Sunday and it has been the memory of Korea that has restored my faith in God.

At the start of our leave, by the way, the Australians disappeared en masse and never returned until the morning we were due to report to the airfield. Going to collect our weapons, it was discovered that an Australian had taken a British No.4 rifle and left his 1914 No.1 Lee Enfield. Technically, of course, there was no real difference as the ammunition used by each rifle was precisely the same. Still, it was an intriguing situation. Quartermasters, as they are, would have blown a fuse at not having the exact specified weapon on their records. War or no War – the records **must** be correct.

Actually, the No.1 rifle would make an interesting trophy in the Regimental Museum and the papers could easily be fiddled but would the Quartermaster stand for it!

CHAPTER TWENTY FOUR

A Time Of Discovery

Following my return from leave, I first found out that I was a member short in my section. After I had departed, Private Shamrock had also made his way down the hill and was next seen fifteen miles in the rear in a state of shock. He was sent to Japan and then to Hong Kong where a rear guard of the regiment was still in control of the camp. When the battalion returned to Hong Kong, I discovered that Shamrock was now a Lance Corporal waiter in the Officers' Mess. He seemed in very good spirits. I rather thought he should have been locked up in a detention barracks. I remembered his remark when he got a bullet through his clothing. "That's enough!" he said. I now knew what he meant and what he had already planned. Even so, there had to be something more to explain his good fortune. It took me a long time to work it out, but then it came to me. Shamrock had talked and talked, but especially about his Platoon Commander who had lain amidst his platoon in a ditch for hours and did nothing about the grenade throwers or the sniper. As Shamrock knew well from World War Two, a failure of an officer had to be covered up at all costs. Lt. Plum was to fail later on in even more spectacular fashion, but it was still covered up.

I was rather interested in other matters that had gone on while I was away and it sparked off a conversation with Private Sprout. "Do you remember that big hill we went up?" I asked. He replied, "We went up a bigger one than that!" I shuddered at the thought and said no more about hills. He then explained how the Company had made the same advance towards the enemy on the very next day. This time though there was no shooting. In the copse they found an abandoned U.S. rifle covered with bloodstains in the spot where I had hit the grenade thrower. I was pleased about that as there is nothing like personal danger to make you hate the enemy.

Carrying on through the copse and up the hill, our chaps found numerous slit trenches but no enemy. However, they did find a treasure of sorts but now without value. Thousands of dollars in American Army script, (This is imitation bank notes for use in American Camps but widely used in South Korea), were found torn up into tiny pieces. When the R.C.T. was ambushed, the Chinese must have had time to search the bodies. Perhaps they thought they might find a way to use the notes, but eventually tore them up.

By the way, while on leave I found out what had happened when I stubbed my stockinged foot on the side of the frozen trench. Having seen my naked feet for the first time in three weeks, I saw the middle toe nail was very black. By the end of the leave, the toe nail had dropped off. It took weeks to grow back again, but I was not prevented from climbing up and down those accursed hills.

Around this time, we had the news that our Brigadier was being replaced on the grounds that he had completed his tour of duty. I wondered at the time why a Brigadier has a fixed tour of duty when the troops under his command just carry on until they are told otherwise. Nearly fifty years later, Colonel Peach told the members of the Regimental Association that one morning the Brigade Staff had found the Brigadier sitting in his Jeep with his hands frozen to the wheel. His mind had gone and he literally could not let go of the wheel. His staff had to force his fingers open and he was carried into his quarters. Within days he was on his way back to the U.K. and eventually an honourable retirement. The strain of command had claimed another victim.

During my childhood and living in Army camps, I was well aware of the condition of shell shock. It was an expression often used in the camps and especially by my Mother. Every one of my Mother's brothers, cousins and brothers-in-law had served in the trenches and all were conscious of the effects of continuous bombardment. In the beginning, those who ran were shot as cowards. Gradually though, it was realised that shell shock was a genuine affliction and steps were taken to treat the casualties as war wounded.

Of course, it was so easy to pretend to be shell shocked that the medical authorities had an awful job separating the fake from the real. Neither was it realised for many years that servicemen could become bomb happy without hearing a shot fired in anger. This applied especially to senior officers. The continual call on their mental resources in warfare had the same effect as shells and bullets – and so our Brigadier succumbed, although it was universally known that he was no coward.

I don't know whether it applied to all of our Brigade but in my regiment in Korea, there was an absolute obsession with the effects of combat fatigue. In general, there was no such condition, or at least it was to be ignored. Under no circumstances was the public to be made aware that some members of the regiment were failing to live up to the normal standard required. It was all "our brave Tommys celebrate with a bottle of beer after a sharp engagement." In reality, there was hardly a person who did not want to leave Korea right away and forever. This applied especially to the National Servicemen and the three year regulars. The countless days and nights of sub-zero weather and the living conditions were the real enemy in Korea. Bullets were only an added annoyance.

Which reminds me of an unexpected pleasure I found while on leave in Tokyo. After the first nights sleep in a proper bed, I pushed back the bedclothes and swung my legs downwards to the floor. I was highly amused. That movement of the legs downwards was a sheer delight. After months of struggling to my feet from a warm (mostly) bed on the frozen ground, the placing of bare feet on a floor was a luxury to be savoured for several minutes. It was little things like this that made our day or marred it in Korea.

When the Brigadier had collapsed, it was our C.O. who had taken over command of the Brigade for a couple of weeks until a new Brigadier was appointed. For us in the lowly ranks, there was no difference in our daily lot. On the C.O.'s return, it was announced that Lt. Col. Peach was to be honoured for his past services by being given command of an offshore stores depot. I could not see where the honour came in for a Lt. Col. with the D.S.O. to be side-tracked to a stores depot from a regiment in the line. In any event, we never saw the Colonel again. It was to be years before the "Die Hards in Korea" said he relinquished command on grounds of ill health. Why oh why could the authorities not say he had succumbed to combat fatigue? After all, he was a genuine hero and had not spared himself one iota when in command. Still, there was the Press to consider and, not least, the American Press.

In any event, during the whole of World War Two, Combat Fatigue was never admitted officially. Instead, the authorities used expressions like "exhaustion" to explain why whole units were sent to the rear with the recommendation that they were not to be used in front line duty ever again. The same principle applied in Korea. There was no such thing as "shell shock" and, consequently, many men and officers continued to serve well beyond their "sell by date", with the result that many fine minds were shattered beyond repair.

Around this time, there was an incident that really put the fear of God into my Company. We had been sent up yet another hill that had been used by the enemy for look out purposes. Before starting the climb, I noticed that some trees had come under fire from some Sabre Jets. I carefully examined one tree in particular and saw that the bullet holes were no more than six inches apart, and also spread in a diamond formation. Anybody in the path of the hail of fire would be hit several times. Anyway, we went up the hill and settled down on the ridge at the summit. No orders were given to dig in, and for that we were extremely grateful, but just to lay in wait for further orders.

We were about a mile from a tremendous battle going on further north. We could only see the explosions of shells and bombs, but quite clearly could see operations of the Sabre Jets. There were usually four jets in formation, and these were controlled by an observation aircraft. This was an older and smaller 'plane that still had a "fan in the front". This observer would make a run over the position and signal to the jets. The Sabres would then make a run over the target but without firing. Once the "all clear" was given by the observer, the jets would come in for real. They would make perhaps three passes at the enemy before going back to base for rearming and refuelling.

The jets did not always have it all their own way. In another incident, I saw a Sabre jet come down with all guns blazing but just simply ploughed straight into the ground. His companions immediately flew off.

Anyway, there we were just sitting around watching when the observer aircraft came roaring over our heads. We had all presumed that the observer was perfectly well aware of our presence and we did not twitch a muscle. The observer came back for another run but we had already put out our recognition panels. These were two long panels made of a silky material. One was coloured blue and the other red. They were placed in the front of the troops in the authorised code of the day. A cross or a 'T' or an 'L' with the colours positioned according to the code. The observer came around for another look and by this time the panel handlers were holding the colours above their heads and were in an open field. We still did not move, and then the Sabres came down for their first blind pass. We still did not run as we just could not believe we were about to be straffed. The jets flew off and did not return. We were very relieved as none of us would have survived! I rather think the pilots were having a bit of a giggle at our expense, but our nerves took another battering.

In this day and age – 2,000 – there is an awful lot written about journalists taking part in various wars. This is all to the good, as the journalists deserve a mention now and then. On the other hand, a lot of their work must be viewed with suspicion. After all, they are writing to please their editors and those who are paying them. We must always keep in mind the French General at the beginning of World War One who said, "The first casualty of war is truth!" Most journalists appear to accept this dictum as their own working policy. I have put in this little diatribe to explain my one and only contact with the Gentlemen of the Press.

We had been doing one of our long marches from Point A to Point B, except we were never told where Point A had been, and even less about Point B, nor the reason why we were on the move. A rest halt had been called and I and my lads were lying in a ditch. It so happened that I was resting next to a sort of paved driveway leading into a field. The field had a gate and both this and the paving were very unusual features in Korea, but I was in no mood or position to appreciate the rarity. It so happened that a group of journalists were standing on the paving and appeared to be expecting something of importance to be happening. It went through my mind that one of the Press Corp might want to have a few words with the hero lying right at their feet. From their conversation, it was obvious the journalists were all British. None, however, were in uniform as accredited Correspondents.

Anyway, the only acknowledgement that several hundred battle scarred warriors were in their immediate vicinity was that one reporter looked down at me in the ditch with an expression of utter distaste. He shuffled his feet closer to his companions. Just then one of the battalion opened the gate and the whole gang of the Press rushed through with the excited cries of that profession who were about to be given a scoop. They headed towards the tent of the Second-in-Command Major Passion Fruit, who was acting C.O. at the time. I never learnt the reason for the journalists' attendance and never saw one of them ever again. This conduct was in complete contrast to the Americans who were constantly publishing interviews with the average G.I. Joe in the field of conflict.

CHAPTER TWENTY FIVE

More Discovery

When we first set foot on the land of the Morning Calm, we British were only faintly aware of the very deep divide between black and white in the American way of life. The blacks were the servants to the whites and that was that. I had my first shock when I was waiting to go on leave to Tokyo. In the morning, I had the need to use a toilet and I went in search of one. I saw the usual canvas structure surrounding the usual portable buckets with wooden seats. What I also saw with a shock was a notice that said "COLOUREDS ONLY!" I did not know what to do so I went in anyway. It was quite a large arrangement and I quickly got settled on the nearest bucket. At the other side were three black soldiers of whom only one was using the facility. They all looked at me in anger but said nothing. It was clearly an embarrassing moment for all of us, and I got out of there as quickly as I could.

Later, I learned that the black fighting soldiers, i.e., infantry of the U.S. Army were all in one R.C.T. the 24th. No white soldier would serve alongside a black man under any circumstances − which brings me to the one and only black soldier in my regiment. He was a reinforcement and by chance was posted to my section. His colour did not disturb any of us, but his personality was one of utter gentleness and a sweet nature. He was unsuited to the army in general, and should never have been in the infantry. Instinctively, the rest of us sought to protect him from the worst of rough living.

One day though we all got a shock. We had spent the night on a hillside only a few feet above a main road. A convoy of trucks was going past and consisted of open two and a half tonners carrying white G.I.s. A shout came from one truck. "Hey! What are your guys doing with that nigger among you? Get him out of there!" Of course, we carried on packing up our gear and pretended not to have heard anything. Later on, when we were getting ready to leave Korea, it was decided that all the reinforcements who had joined us since January 1951 would be transferred to our relieving battalion, the King's Shropshire Light Infantry. I and several others made it known to the officers that our "pet blackie" should come back with the regiment to Hong Kong. Thankfully it was agreed it had been the usual mistake by otherwise well meaning authorities to have posted "Blackie" to Korea anyway.

Another incident that gave us a mild shock of surprise was our one and only meeting up with a portion of the 29th Brigade. We were going from A to B and had been marching for several miles and, as usual, were loaded up to the eyeballs. A huge battle was taking place about half a mile north of us and on our left. Being thoroughly exhausted by this time, we were not really interested in the fighting. After all, it was someone else's affair. Just then we came upon a number of tanks parked by the side of the road. There was a high bank on our left. We were marching to the east by the way. A number of tank crews (British) were clambering up the bank to watch the spectacle and I have no doubt it was interesting, but we were very, very tired. I was leading our Company and I managed to wave a cheery hello to the "tankies" and I think one or two others managed to do the same. Otherwise the whole battalion passed through in dead silence.

By the look on the faces of those tank crews, it was obvious that they were surprised by our complete indifference to our surroundings. I also suppose that we hammed it up a bit, but we were genuinely in no mood to do anything but press on to our objective and get some well earned rest.

Watching the Olympics on the tv I am always struck by the never ending speeches by the athletes of bringing their bodies up to tip top performance for their big day. We in the 27th Brigade had several times reached our peak and then stayed there without rest. As a consequence, we were always exhausted. Whenever we woke up our bodies were already stretched to their limit. When we started to dig in our bodies were screaming for relief before we had lifted a pick. We were tired, tired, tired all the time and these days never moved an inch unless under orders or of necessity.

In spite of all our troubles though, we still managed a lot of laughter and joking around the all important camp fires. These fires were kept going all the time when we were not on the move. They were the life line we clung to in order to avoid a complete collapse of morale.

In another incident of this period, we were woken up at three in the morning to give a hand to the Australians who were in danger of being over run by the enemy. We were ready to move in twenty minutes. It had long been the practise (which we had taught ourselves) to have every item packed away in our equipment once its use was over. Mess tins and spoons for instance – once we had finished with the specific tool, it was returned to its proper place. Once our bedding was laid down for the night, then equipment, boots and weapons were laid alongside in an exact order. We were then able to rise, put on our boots and roll up the bedding in the darkness. Our weapons were picked up last, and we were ready, knowing that nothing had been left behind.

We formed up on the road and marched off for a walk of about twelve miles. In ordinary training schedules this march would take about four hours, but we always had this massive weight hanging all over our body. By the time we arrived at our destination, the day was well advanced. We were to dig a line of trenches going from a small hill on our left to a village on our right. Strangely enough, the village was still occupied by the inhabitants although they remained battened down the whole time we were there. Only two of our companies were involved in this move, or at least we just did not know where the rest of the battalion were at the time. Apparently, the enemy were on the far side of a wide valley and in distance of about half a mile. We were to wait for an onslaught of bugle blowing Chinese.

The order was given that we were to adopt a position of all round defence. If a platoon was all on its own, then two sections would face the enemy and the third section would face towards the rear with Platoon H.Q. in the middle. Lt. Plum duly instructed his Section Commanders according to the order, but did not allow for us being in company with five other platoons. We finished up with our rear section facing another platoon about ten yards away. Even that platoon got it wrong. They should all have been facing to the rear, but had also adopted the all round defence tactic. Consequently, we had British squaddies face to face with loaded weapons, but also laughing at each other and at the laughable hiatus. As nobody came from Company H.Q. to sort things out, that's the way we remained.

The digging took all day, but at sunset we still had not got down to a comfortable depth. At best we stood up with the trench barely thigh high. In my own trench, we had a problem with a huge boulder but once my mate and I had heaved it away we had our trench. We also had another setback by finding the body of a six month old child. It had been buried about six inches below the surface of the ground and was wrapped in a small blanket. My pick had penetrated some soft earth, and I went carefully until I made the discovery. I put the bundle to one side and carried on digging. When we left the next day, the bundle was still there but I presumed the villagers would now carry out an even deeper burial in my trench.

The situation with the enemy was deemed so serious that a fifty per cent stand to was ordered. This meant that the Platoon Commander and the Sergeant also took their turn in the trenches and for the first time in the campaign. The first watch went on about ten o'clock and were to stay on their feet for four hours. We were so exhausted that we kept falling asleep with our knees braced against the side of the trench. First I would nod off and Private Sprout would dig me in the ribs to wake me up. Three or four minutes later Sprout would be nodding off. It would then be my turn to shake him about a bit. This went on for four hours. In addition, our eyeballs felt as though needles were being pushed in and out.

I was on the first shift and so I was meant to get four hours sleep before general stand to at six o'clock a.m. I found that in my state of exhaustion I was unable to sleep properly and kept waking up. I suppose I had no more than two hours sleep at the most. The dawn came and we had not seen the Chinese hordes. We had breakfast and changed down the number of sentries. During the day, we caught up on our sleep in stretches of about an hour at a time. We left that part of the line late in the afternoon but it had been yet another very, very bad day.

We had been in Korea for about six months, but I can't say that I had ever been deep down frightened. Not the paralysing type that prevents a man from being unable to move. Nervous, scared, yes – but I was always able to make an appreciation of the situation and give orders. I suppose my training had helped there and being in command of troops and compelled to set an example was of enormous value. The soldier who has only himself to consider is always the most vulnerable to fright and later I appreciated my luck in having stripes on my arm.

About this time we became aware that we had a new Commanding Officer. Why the Second-in-Command had not been promoted to the vacancy remains a mystery. Anyway, the new chap had been in charge of some stores depot in Japan, but had extracted a promise from the General Officer-in-Command that he would get the first vacancy for a Lt./Col. in the Brigade. This happened to be us and so he came. Not that we in the rifle companies ever had a visit from him. Incidentally, when the last Major had collapsed, we never had a replacement. Captain Orange, the Second-in-Command, took over as Company Commander and that's the way it stayed. He was never even given the temporary rank of Major to make up for his responsibilities. One of the subalterns was made Second-in-Command but he wasn't made a temporary Captain either. This sort of procedure was typical not only in my regiment but in the Brigade generally. Everything was carried out on a shoe string basis. Economy was the watchword, even when men were dead or dying.

Yet another incident that caused us to be even more tired was one that was deemed to be unnecessary by all those involved. My Company was advancing on a broad front through a very wide valley. Our three platoons were advancing in line together when the order came to stop where we were and dig in. This was about ten in the morning, and we just got on with the now hated chore. The work progressed very well, and when we stopped for our midday meal we even had a bottle of beer each. After the meal was finished, we had another order, and that was to retreat for about three hundred yards. Having gone back down the valley and settled in our positions, we then had to dig in again.

The new trench system took another four hours of back breaking toil and no sooner had we finished than we had a new order to move forward again. But it was not back to our first row of trenches but a few hundred yards further on. Another order came to dig in and at this Sgt. Swede went berserk. He swore mightily and loudly and eventually was sent to the rear under open arrest. The rest of us just had to dig another trench system, but this one was a very sketchy affair. Merely a scrape in the ground, but it could not be helped as we were dead beat. When Sgt. Swede went to the rear I was made temporary Platoon Sergeant, but I merely went back to my section and stayed with them. If I had any duties to perform, I forgot all about them in my state of fatigue.

Sgt. Swede came back the next day and matters went on as before. There appeared to be no tactical reason why we went back and forth. I rather think the acting Company Commander was just being bloody minded and seeking to assert his authority. This sort of behaviour made no difference to the War whatsoever. We were not in contact with the enemy and in no danger. I rather think it was the case of not allowing the troops to be idle.

CHAPTER TWENTY SIX

Unrewarded Gallantry

In another incident, I earned the award of the Victoria Cross but did not even get a Mention-in-Dispatches. There were reasons for this omission and they were :- One: I did not get killed. Two: Nobody else was killed. Three: Several hundred of my colleagues were ashamed of their own conduct in the affair.

It happened like this. The whole battalion were advancing through a very broad valley with two companies in line abreast and the other two companies forming a second line in the rear. Battalion Headquarters were in between the lines but on the right hand side of the valley where there was a road. We had paused for a rest, and it so happened I was the extreme left hand man of the front line, i.e. the furthest from Headquarters. I was idly watching events and saw a messenger leave H.Q. and contact my Platoon Commander. He in turn came to me and said, "Come with me! The C.O.'s got a job for you." I followed him to the H.Q. group feeling extremely flattered.

I had automatically called my section after me and the rest of the platoon had followed. On arrival at the hallowed ground occupied by the C.O. (actually the Second-in-Command) and his group, I was handed a pair of binoculars and told to observe an enemy entrenchment about three hundred yards away and up a slope. The trench was at the apex of a triangle with the base being on the road and about fifty yards wide. As the ground went up it narrowed to about six feet. The whole set up was at right angles to the road. I took the binoculars and had a look. The trench was covered over and from the slit protruded a barrel of a machine gun. The C.O. said, "I want you to go up there and have a look around."

I rather felt like applying for my discharge-by-purchase right there and then. Instead, of course, I just nodded politely and lined up my lads on either side of me. It was all done by signals as I could not speak for the moment. I started off and went up the ravine for about fifty yards and then stopped. Already my lads were lagging twenty yards behind me. I gave an angry wave for them to close up and went on for another fifty yards. I stopped again and looked back and my section were now forty yards behind me. No amount of waving or shouting could get them any nearer.

But I also saw the rest of the Platoon following on. By the way – we were all fully laden with the habitual equipment rations and ammunition. Making a mad dash for it was out of the question. I went now for about a hundred yards with the ravine walls closing in towards me with banks about eight feet high. There wasn't a scrap of cover. I took another look back and saw the whole Company were in the ravine but hugging the sides for comfort. I was almost dead with fright but went forward another fifty yards. That machine gun was pointing dead at my chest. Any bullets fired would have to go through me before anyone else was in danger. I took another look back and saw the whole Company were lying flat and now a hundred yards away. In addition, one hundred pairs of eyes were looking at me and me alone.

I wanted so much to retreat but those eyes in my back prevented any such nonsense. Not now would I go back even an inch. But at the same time I could not stay where I was. By now I could see into the entrenchment but there was no movement whatsoever. I wondered why the enemy had not opened fire. They could have easily accounted for half the Company with one belt of ammo. I drew a deep breath and charged up the hill for the last remaining fifty yards. Jumping over the machine gun, I landed on a small circular plateau. I could see instantly that there were other slit trenches around the edge. I ran a quarter way round the plateau to my left. I turned and ran back and over the machine gun and went a quarter way round to the right. There were just empty trenches. I walked slowly back to the subject in question.

I thought about booby traps but I bent down and took hold of the barrel. I swung it over my head to show the whole battalion I was waving a broom handle.

There came a rousing cheer from below and one hundred heroes rose to their feet and charged up the hill to get to grips with the long gone enemy. There was much hustle and bustle and orders were given to dig in once again. Not one of those comrades spoke a word to me or looked me in the eye. A few minutes later two subalterns, who I had never seen before, walked past me. They were not carrying any arms or equipment and could not go very far. One said to the other, "I knew it was that all the time!" I wondered about that remark and was tempted to ask why they had not led the way up the hill. The subalterns turned round and went back down the ravine. It was a long time before I got the message. I was not to get any recognition for my feat as too many officers were only too willing to let me get killed on my own.

A little while later, another Platoon Commander from my Company came to me and virtually ordered me to lead one of his sections in searching some woodland for possible enemy. This search had been ordered by the O.C. of the Company but I believe that his own NCOs had suggested I perform the operation. Neither Lt. Plum or Sgt. Swede made any objections. The other Lt. was smiling all the time and I still don't know why the peculiar instruction was made. I was still shaking with fright but I went along. I formed up some of the men from the other Platoon and led them in line through the woods. We did not have to go far before coming to the edge of some bare hillside. The Lt. came with me and was still smiling. We returned and I went back to my own position. I am still unaware of the purpose of that little exercise. Perhaps it was to show me that there never was any enemy there after all. That still does not explain why the whole Company were lying flat in the ravine with grey faces and staring eyes, and that included the officers.

We dug in and I slowly recovered.

A couple of days later, we were making another sweep up yet another valley and at about mid day were ordered to dig in yet again. The officers were called to a conference with Capt. Orange which only lasted a few minutes. Lt. Plum returned in a state of high anxiety. Apparently the enemy had used aircraft against some forward troops and defensive measures had to be taken. In future, slit trenches had to include overhead cover. Lt. Plum spoke only to me and, hardly able to speak, ordered me to ensure that overhead cover was built immediately. Now this cover required pieces of wood or corrugated sheeting to be laid across the trench and earth piled on top. Or a very deep trench was dug with bolt holes hacked out of the sides.

There were two snags to the situation. One was that we had no idea how long we were to stay in that position and, two, the valley was absolutely devoid of any fences or structures of any kind. All we had was grass and paddy fields. Nonetheless we had to do something. Lt. Plum was going out of his mind with fear of the enemy and of the C.O. I went to my section and ordered them to start digging yet again. We went down another six inches and left it at that. Lt. Plum never came back and, in any event, we moved on the next morning. Thankfully aircraft cover was never mentioned again. It was just something that the division had to pass on downwards in order to cover their backs. Certainly in my case I never saw any enemy aircraft during the campaign and I don't think any other ground troops did either.

This order was typical of many that were passed down from on high. It was all "just in case" and regardless of the condition or comfort of the common soldier. Though to be fair to the high command, our battalion was quite a nuisance factor in the higher scheme of things. We were supposed to return to Hong Kong in October 1950 and again in December but here we were still. Nobody really knew what to do with us as all the plans revolved around the 29th Brigade which had been formed up in Colchester for the specific purpose of representing the British Army in the Korean War. We of the 27th Brigade were the Cinderellas and we had no chance of going to the Ball!

Then came our big chance. We were to take over a series of hills which in general was called Billingsgate as all the hills were named Salmon, Sardine, Dab, etc. At this stage I give the reader fair warning that my account of the next seven days is at variance with the passages relating to the battle given in "The Die-hards in Korea", especially regarding dates. The chap who edited the various notes many years after the events was at one time my Company Commander, but had left the battalion some months before to go on a goodwill tour of America. Of course, my story of Korea revolves around me and I maintain my account is more accurate. The "Official" accounts tend to gloss over some very important events and for reasons which I have already made obvious.

The hills we were to ascend were two high ridges on either side of a very deep ravine. The left hand ridge had already been attempted by two of our companies, but they were driven back with casualties. A second attempt found them pinned down half way along the left hand ridge. My Company went up the right hand side and we met no opposition whatsoever. Neither did we see any sign that the enemy had been there before us.

When we first made a road march before actually starting the climb most of us saw our new C.O. for the first time. His driver of the U.S. Jeep had parked on a piece of grassy bank slightly higher than the dusty road and the C.O. was standing to one side. He was dressed in some sort of combination uniform but the most striking item were his boots. I think they were American based but they shone like glass. Brown in colour but very highly glazed. Without doubt they really were magnificent with the sheen of French Polishing. The C.O. did not move an inch while we marched past and had only to take one sideways step into his seat. He gave the impression that his boots were of far more importance than the men marching past to their possible deaths.

As far as our ridge went, it was a thing of beauty and a joy to behold. It was heavily wooded and that meant twigs to heat up our cans of food. In fact, there was so much fallen branches we were able to keep a fire going all day. This fire became the focal point of daily life for seven days and because it was still very cold, only the sentries were absent from the cheery glow. Rations and water were brought up on a daily basis by Korean porters, and when we had erected our Pup tents and spread out our bedding our heaven was complete – almost!

Our ridge extended for about three hundred yards and then stopped at a huge hole which was shaped like a champagne glass. A narrow rim tapering down even closer to the bottom. The sides of the hole were very steep and went down and down and down. Further round the rim were Canadian troops but between us we only occupied twenty five per cent of the rim. In fact, half of the rim wasn't there. It was just as if the glass had been dropped and one side of the flute was now missing. The Chinese occupied a ridge on that side but were maybe half a mile away. In between was "NO MANS LAND". As I said, two companies were on the top of our hill but facing us across the valley was a ridge occupied by the Chinese. Our two companies on the other side were about two hundred yards lower than us and for the moment unable to advance any higher.

And then, just as we were feeling quite happy, the situation changed. We were under fire from a sniper who was dug in on the forward slope of the Chinese ridge. He fired only once about every twenty or thirty minutes, but we were forced to keep down under cover which was rather annoying. The sniper was about five hundred yards away as the crow flies, but his shots were getting close as time went on. I had done a Snipers' Course at Warminster and knew something about the art. For accuracy, the sniper needed to zero in – that is, he had to see the strike of the shot and adjust the sights accordingly. On a rifle range this could be done on a target with a marker indicating the strike. In the field, the sniper did not have this advantage and needed to see a body keel over before he was certain of the adjustments made. I almost assisted the enemy sniper with his sight setting. After the evening meal and while it was still light, I decided to have a look across the valley at the enemy positions. With stupid bravado I walked upright and stood on the top of the ridge with open sky behind me. Within thirty seconds I felt a thud in my left foot. I looked down and saw a bullet had scored a groove along the outside of the heel of my boot. With even more stupid bravado, I turned slowly and casually rejoined my section. I could have jumped a mile high and run but I felt I had been outsmarted and I was very indignant. I showed my comrades my near miss and warned them to keep below the crest. Not that they needed any warning!

My foot smarted for about three days, but I never thought of reporting it to anyone.

CHAPTER TWENTY SEVEN

Another Victory

We were on the series of hills called Billingsgate for seven days and each day came under fire from one source or another and of one type or another. These I will describe as I go along. When I say we though, I am being generous to my comrades. On one occasion the enemy fire was directed to me alone.

While we were up on the ridge the Canadian Field Artillery kept up a barrage towards the enemy positions on a fairly regular basis. We didn't mind this even though the Canadians could only just clear the ridge. Two or three times the salvos went over so low that some shells hit the trees and exploded over our heads. This was not nice at all but there were no reports of any injuries, and so we put up with it.

On the second day I was rather indignant about the sniper who nearly saw me off and decided to do something about it. I never consulted Lt. Plum or Sgt. Swede but simply took one of our L.M.G.'s and some bandoleers of ammunition and took up a position on the far right of our ridge. I also took along Pte. Pea who, as ever, was only too willing to join in the fun. A few days prior to this, one of our lads had filched a pair of binoculars from an unguarded U.S. Jeep. I borrowed the binoculars as well. I set up the Bren gun under a bush and set out to find the sniper's position. He was very obliging and started taking pot shots at me and Pea right away. I spent some time searching a large bare area of ground on the enemy's forward slope as I felt this was where the shots were coming from. I was correct in this assumption.

The sniper was operating from two small dugouts with roof covering. His firing apertures were only just big enough to poke through his rifle, fire a shot, and withdraw. This is where the sniper made a mistake. Had he constructed a larger dugout, where he could lie down with his rifle poking through some shrubbery, we may never have found him. It was the movement between the two apertures that was his downfall. He would push out his rifle, focus the sight and fire and withdraw, all in three seconds or less. I must admit that, as a sniper, the enemy soldier was superb. Firing from about five hundred yards away, he was getting his shots very, very close. The biggest snag with operating a sniper's rifle is the focusing of the scope. You are looking through two or more sets of glass lenses which are lined up so that there is a clear picture; then you have to move the whole thing until you have the cross hairs on the target — then fire!

As one example of how difficult this is, I point out that twice I won the Sniper Championship at Bisley in later years and each time only hit the target seven times out of ten shots. Each exposure of the target is for three seconds only and the target comes into view in a different position each time. Between Bisley and Korea, it was about equal in degrees of difficulty for the sniper and myself.

When I set up the Bren gun under some overhanging shrubbery, I had to make it obvious to the sniper what I was doing. I did not know where he was, but I had to attract his fire. He obliged in short order. I soon spotted the two dugouts and showed Private Pea where they were. He kept a lookout through the binoculars while I let loose with some very short bursts. It was Pte. Pea's job to let me know where my shots were going in relation to the targets. Pretty soon, we established that the shots were going six feet high and two feet right. Luckily, I was able to pick out two aiming marks. One was a tin can, six feet low and two feet left of the apertures. We then got the party going. The higher aperture was named 'One' and the other 'Two'.

While Pte. Pea looked through the binoculars for movement, I focused the sights roughly between the two aiming marks. Once movement was spotted – and this would be the sniper rifle being pushed out – Pea would call out 'One' or 'Two' as the case may be, and I would focus and fire a short burst. Pea gladly pointed out that my shots were getting very close to the apertures. The sniper's shots though were also getting close. One broke off a twig over my head. Another burrowed into the ground between the legs of the Bren. Others whined around my head. After an hour, I gave Pea a spell on the Bren while I spotted. Pea also did a very good job. After half an hour, I took over the Bren again but within twenty or thirty minutes there was no fire being returned by the sniper. Just then, Sgt. Swede came along with the complaint that I was using up all the Platoon ammunition. I was choked I must say. The whole object of our presence in Korea was to carry the fight to the enemy. Or at least that was my way of thinking. Anyway, Pea and I packed up and rejoined the section. I had the smug satisfaction of noting that no more shots came from that sniper towards the Platoon and we were all able to move about more freely. By way of thanks, I was met with the usual silence.

That night and all the next day was uneventful except for one surprising happening. Each day on the ridge, water and rations were brought up by Korean porters under the direction of the Colour Sergeant. This day though, the controlling officer was none other than the Battalion Quartermaster. He was, of course, over the age of forty and it must have been quite an effort. The next day, the controlling officer was the Regimental Quartermaster Sergeant, (Warrant Officer Class ii), and also around forty years of age. There was no military reason why either of these gentlemen should trawl all the way up to our ridge, but they seemed to be hugging themselves with delight. Later it turned out that they already knew that the Regiment was being pulled out of the line in about three or four days in readiness for shipment to Hong Kong. The day trip up the ridge was merely to claim time at the sharp end.

While we are on the subject of the Quartermaster, I am reminded that while we were on the ridge, one of our lads tore a large hole through his U.S. Combat trousers and also his British Battledress trousers. This must have been difficult to accomplish, but there it was. Replacements were asked for and the reply came back that the criminal concerned would have to pay for the malicious damage – this to a chap who had worn these garments day and night for seven months in very arduous conditions and while under fire. It took the intervention of the C.O. to ensure that the replacements should be issued without charge.

I think it was on our third night that we had a rude interruption to our fairly peaceful life. A couple of shots were fired from the bottom of the wine glass. Two companies were instantly awake and putting on our boots and grabbing our weapons, we stood to and all this without saying a word. The wine glass I might explain was a very deep hole at the end of our ridge, but with one side, nearest the Chinese, cut away as though a wine glass had been dropped and one sliver had been broken off. No troops occupied this part of the line as the sides of the hole were very steep and the ground littered with frozen twigs under the snow which was now melting. A quarter of the way round the wine glass and the ground was occupied by Canadian troops who stopped short of the cut away portion of the glass.

After a little while word came from the other Company Commander that a patrol must be sent out to find out what was what. My platoon was nearest and automatically I was selected as the patrol leader. Detailing three of my chaps who I felt it was their turn for the project, I set off down the glass. The twigs underfoot made an awful racket, but I pressed on down. On the way, I wondered if we were going into a trap. We were about half way down when a single shot was fired, but this time from the valley floor on the Chinese side. The ground stretched for half a mile from the glass to the ridge, occupied by the Gooks. I thought may be this was an extension of the trap; the enemy pretending to be on their way back, but leaving an ambush. I went down further still and now the flute was getting very narrow. Another shot was fired and this was much nearer to the Chinese ridge. Were they just playing with us, I wondered. Needless to say, my nerves were stretched like banjo strings.

A few yards more and almost in sight of the bottom of the glass, and I heard another fearsome noise. There was yelling and shooting from up above. It was the Canadians who had by now decided to have a look see. They were very sensible though. They forged down the side of the glass, shooting as they went, and making a racket. It was extremely unlikely that any ambush party would stay around in the circumstances. But I now had a further problem. Was I now going to wait at the bottom of the glass and politely introduce myself? I took half a second to decide I was not going to be polite in any circumstances. I turned and waved to the patrol to retreat, but as quickly as we could. While we were going back up the slope, the Canadians reached the bottom of the glass and indulged in an orgy of shooting. From the sounds of things, they did not find any Chinese, which was hardly surprising.

My companions and I crept up to our tents and expected a volley of shots to follow us, but that never happened, luckily. I might add at this time that although it was now about three a.m. we could see enough to know what was going on. For months we had operated without any man made light whatsoever, and moving at night was for us now just a normal accomplishment.

I looked around for somebody to report to. There was nobody. Not a Major, a Captain, a Lieutenant or a Sergeant. Only the sentries. I and my patrol went to our tents and to sleep. In the morning, I arose and set about preparing my breakfast. Not even Lt. Plum came to make enquiries in spite of all the shooting that went on during the night. I and my patrol could have been wiped out by the Chinese, or the Canadians, but there was a total lack of interest. I and my section were chatting around the section fire when Pte. Carrot, our Bren Gunner, asked, "What shot? What shooting?" The rest of us were stunned into silence. Now Carrot was always a bit of a skiver and would be reluctant to get out of his bed, but it was obvious that he was genuinely unaware of what had been going on. I on my part had never checked that all of my section had stood to. It was unthinkable that there was a person who had not heard that first shot from the bottom of the wine glass. But there it was. Pte. Carrot had not heard a thing. Not even the scrambling of his tent mate. Not even the orders to form a patrol or the return of that patrol. In civvie street Carrot was a hard case and now in Korea he was just the same.

It was the fifth day, I think, when it was decided to withdraw the two companies from the left hand ridge and to replace them with my Company. I think it was the Canadians who replaced us, but I am not sure. Anyway, we went over to the other ridge by way of the valley in between. It meant going down a long way and up again, but we passed the sniper's position on the forward. The ground was a mass of bullet holes from the Bren gun bursts but they centred in on the two dug outs. One of our chaps said, "That's from a Vickers (Medium Machine Gun) but I did not bother to correct him. I did, however, have a look inside and found a Chinese cap and a blood stained bandage. There was no rifle, of course, but neither were there any cartridge cases but the Chinese had a habit of collecting these up before withdrawing. Silently, I marked myself down for a hit.

As we were going up a path to the other ridge, we met the acting C.O. coming down. He took a hard look at me and said something to my Company Commander. It was in reference to my growth of beard. In 'C' Company we had only each day enough water to drink and make coffee and cocoa. Washing and shaving was out of the question. I heard no more of the matter as the whole Company was in the same condition. On arriving at our new position, we discovered that the other Company had continual running water from a spring. No doubt there was washing and shaving at least every other day.

CHAPTER TWENTY EIGHT

A Great Relief

When we arrived on top of the other ridge, the other Company had already withdrawn, but we noticed that there were no slit trenches dug, which was very surprising to us in 'C' Company. Actually there were some slit trenches but these had been dug by the Chinese. One of these surprisingly had a shovel leaning to the side of the trench. It was a good shovel and unbroken. A temptation for anyone! Closer inspection revealed a thin wire leading from just underneath the handle to some repacked earth. Obviously the wire led to a grenade with the pin out. Nobody had taken a chance and the booby trap was still there when we left.

Before we could do anything more, orders came for an attack on a Chinese position. This position was manned by just two enemy soldiers, but for us it was a virtual death trap. The enemy had constructed a dugout with roofing and they faced just two avenues of approach up the hill. For the enemy it was also suicidal as they had no means of getting away.

By the way, I was no longer in possession of my U.S. Carbine. Before we had gone up the first ridge, I was sent for by somebody assisting the Colour Sergeant, and told I must take back my Sten gun and magazines from the truck where I had left them. I was rather annoyed, but took the Sten gun and left in its place the U.S. Carbine. When we first arrived on the other ridge Lt. Plum and Sgt. Swede had gone all the way to the bottom and then returned. Lt. Plum was trying to hide it but he was now armed with my carbine. He smirked at Sgt. Swede as they passed me but that incident wiped out any respect I had for Plum as either an Officer and a Gentleman. The next time I saw that carbine was in the Garrison Guard Room in Hong Kong where it was held with other arms belonging to the Garrison Staff. Incidentally, Plum was now Second-in-Command of the Detention Barracks and part of Garrison Headquarters.

Anyway, back to the Battle of Billingsgate where Lt. Pear and his Platoon had been ordered to attack the Chinese dugouts. So twenty five men were trying to wipe out just two of the enemy. They had a very hard job. The Platoon had occupied a small half circular ridge which actually overlooked the Chinese position. The Platoon were firing their arms and throwing grenades at the Chinese, who were actually only twenty yards away, if that. The Chinese were returning fire with a sub-machine and stun grenades. These stun grenades caused little physical damage, but exploded with a shattering roar. I rather feel they were designed for civilian riot control rather than a battlefield, but the enemy seemed to have an enormous amount of them in the dugout.

Lt. Plum had been ordered to attack the Chinese from our left. Plum's answer to the problem was to lie down where he was and to send forward a section to have a look see. They duly went forward and were seen to be milling around some bushes at the side of a huge rock. In desperation I went forward to have a look for myself. I was stunned and very scared with what I saw. Funnily enough, I never saw the other Section Leader or his Second-in-Command. There were half a dozen men bobbing in and out of the bushes which were growing on the left hand side of a narrow path. On the right hand side was a sheer cliff going up for about twenty feet. By the way, the bushes hid another sheer cliff going downwards. Only one man could advance at a time and that was straight under the guns and grenades of the enemy. An impossible task for anyone but as Lt. Plum never got to his feet, he was not aware of the situation. He just lay there urging on the other section.

I left Point Suicide and went to join Lt. Pear's Platoon on the ridge. Lt. Pear gave a cheerful smile in acknowledgement and carried on with directing the fire. I took up a position on the left of his Platoon and opened up with my Sten gun. I could see a ferocious pair of eyes looking at me from the dugout and became aware that bursts of fire were coming my way. This situation lasted only a very short time as there were several enormous explosions. Further up the hill and about five hundred yards away was yet another Chinese dugout. Two men again were firing at us with rifles but with no effect. The U.S. Artillery with 155s (medium artillery) had been ordered to sort out this other nuisance. The resulting shells fell all around us with mind numbing effect. Like a Corky the Cat cartoon, I felt the ground recede from underneath me, and then come back and hit me with a thump. Of course, actually it was the reverse. I had been lifted up several inches and thumped back on the ridge.

The explosions stirred up the dust to a height of about two feet. I waited for the fog to clear and saw a figure scrambling up the side of the dugout. An attempt to get away, I thought. I fired a burst and the figure dropped down and below my sight. I could not see any more movement and there was now silence.

A couple of minutes later, Sgt. Swede came up the slope and told me that Lt. Plum had been led away by the hand. He was crying and saying he "couldn't take any more!" There amidst the battle I felt an enormous relief sweep over me. I never spoke a word but I was overjoyed. I was happy beyond all understanding. No longer would I have to cover up for this very poor specimen of a leader. I rejoined the Platoon and, for want of other orders, we went back a couple of hundred yards and rested.

Then a junior NCO came down from the ridge with a message for Company H.Q.'s. In passing he told us that 2/Lt. Pear had been wounded. A stretcher party came down from the scene of battle carrying the casualty. (I took a photograph of this.) We could see that 2/Lt. was lying face down and later we were told he had been hit in the back. I could not see how this could have happened as, when I was with that Platoon, the Leader was determinedly facing the enemy. Later still it was implied that the casualty had been hit by shrapnel from the American shelling. Eventually, Pear was shipped to Japan where an operation was performed and we were all shocked to learn that the missile was a British 9mm bullet. It is quite possible, of course, that the Chinese could have been using this type of ammunition. We British had supplied many nations with arms and ammunition during World War Two and not least the Chinese who were fighting the Japanese and the Koreans in Burma and elsewhere.

But when the stretcher party went past me, I was given some very pointed looks. I was puzzled to say the least. Then it occurred to me that 2/Lt. Pear had been wearing some sort of calf coloured leather waistcoat over his combat jacket. This waistcoat was a very expensive gift from his wife and was acquired in London. When I had fired at the man scrambling up the side of the dugout, he was also wearing a calf coloured jacket. But when I fired at the enemy soldier, 2/Lt. Pear was lying down on the ridge and was something like ten yards from me on my right hand side. Had I been spun round at right angles by the shelling and mistakenly shot 2/Lt. Pear? I knew in my heart this wasn't so but for forty nine years I have lived with the unspoken accusation that I shot a comrade.

Now at last I have worked out the real solution and eased my mind considerably. When the shelling occurred, all of us on that ridge were bounced up and down again with considerable force. I now conclude that it was another Corporal, of that Platoon, who had loosed off a shot from a Sten gun into the kidney of 2/Lt. Pear. That explains why there was great reluctance for anyone of the Platoon to talk about the wounding. 2/Lt. Pear died two months later with his wife at his bedside. I dearly wish that anyone reading this book will finally tell the truth. There is hardly going to be a Court Martial from an accidental shot.

But back again to the Battle of Billingsgate. My Platoon now under the command of Sgt. Swede, were about three hundred yards from the enemy and 2/Lt. Pear's Platoon, also under command of a Sgt. had been withdrawn back even further. The Chinese were still in possession of the ridge and with no more than four men forming the defence. Two men in "our" dugout, and two more further up the hill. In the meantime, the Australians had been sent for to take over the task at which we had so miserably failed. At this point, I must take umbrage with our Company Commander, Capt. Orange. At no time whatsoever did he show himself to the Company. He executed authority by sending messages forward to the Platoon.

It would be thought that, at the loss of two Platoon Commanders, he would go forward to find out what was going on. He never did then, nor later.

While we were "resting" the Australians came through our position and went forward to the enemy dugout. As soon as they arrived, there was an order to fix bayonets and, "Come on lads!" and the whole lot charged without bothering with things like covering fire. We heard the yells, the thud of the stun grenades, some rifle and sub machine gun fire and the silence. In five minutes the "Aussies" had done what we had failed to do in five days. I felt deeply humiliated even though I had no reason to blame myself for anything. While we were still resting, one of the Australians came towards us. He had no equipment or rifle and no head-dress. His face was pockmarked with tiny particles of powder from a stun grenade. He was volatile and could not stay still but he made good sense. I asked him how many bodies were in the dugout. He replied, "I don't know. We just pulled them out and threw them down the hill." He then went on down for further medical attention.

We stayed where we were for that night and then moved onto the ridge formerly occupied by 'B' Company. We then found out why Major Passion Fruit was so annoyed with 'C' Co.'s beards. 'B' Company had a constant supply of cold, clear running water. The Chinese had obviously found the spring first and had fixed up a horizontal pipe from which poured forth the precious liquid. We all washed and shaved that day but we had grown quite used to our stubble and felt it increased our manly stature. We messed about a bit with digging slit trenches and then came a shout. "Hey! There's some shelling!" I wandered over towards the chap's yelling and, true enough, we were under shell fire. In a wooded area about quarter of a mile away we could see the explosions coming from Chinese guns. The sound reached us much later than the sighting.

From my training in Germany, I surmised the guns were being fired at maximum range. This was probably true as we only had two salvos and then there were no more. The effect of the gun fire was not yet over though. Some men from another platoon came to me and said, "Come and look at Beetroot!" Now Beetroot had been in my section in the early days of Korea, but there had been a sorting out of numbers. In fact, I had one too many for a rifle section and somebody else was one short. I had instructions to export one of my riflemen. I chose Beetroot because he was a simpleton and a devout coward. At only a suggestion of gun fire he would grovel on the ground and whimper. The other men would have nothing to do with him. He even had to sleep by himself.

I had heard that when we first climbed up the ridge of Billingsgate, Beetroot had to be dragged up with rifle slings around his waist. Anyway, I went to have a look. Beetroot was curled up in a ball at the bottom of a trench and was refusing to come out. He looked up at me and whimpered, "I'm sorry, John. I'm sorry!" I looked at him for a few seconds and then walked away. I was annoyed. This Platoon still had a Subaltern and a Sergeant and three Corporals but the lads came to me first. This had been the way of things since we first landed in Pusan. I don't know why, but there it was. About half an hour later I saw Beetroot being carried down the hill on a stretcher. He was a three year Regular by the way. He had signed on for the extra pay and leave. Like many other three year Regulars, Korea came as an almighty shock.

Even so, there was something I did not like about the situation with Beetroot cowering in the bottom of the trench.

It just did not feel right. In normal circumstances, any gun fire would make men blanche and tremble, but they would all automatically hide their fears from each other. Anything, rather than be called a cowardy, cowardy custard. I knew only too well my own feelings at such times. In the case of this particular shelling, it was a flash of amusement and gave us an excuse for laughter, and it was a badly needed relief from the ever present danger; but not for Beetroot who took every opportunity to show his cowardice. As I said, there was something not quite right on this particular day.

CHAPTER TWENTY NINE

The Leaders and the Led

Warfare brings out the best and the worst in all of us but, just as the worst was hidden from Public view, so was the best deliberately overlooked.

But I must get back to the main story. We got on with cleaning ourselves up and also rejoiced at the weak sunshine. Life was almost bearable for a change. The next day, we were relieved by a whole Regimental Combat Team of South Koreans. In other words, three men took over from one! Not that we cared. We were going to get a rest and it was actually at the rear. The common conception of being in reserve is that the unit actually marches away from the front and towards rest and relaxation. Once my battalion was at the top of a hill and holding a place in the front line. The next day we were told that we were now in Brigade Reserve. The following day, we were in Divisional Reserve and the day after that in Corps Reserve. We never actually moved a single inch, but who were we to question our superiors! In real terms, we put out the same sentries and ate the same food and had the normal amount of sleep.

We were now leaving Billingsgate and actually leaving Korea although this last was passed on in whispers. On the way down, we passed the spot where we had last seen our C.O. Lo and behold, there he was again! Standing by his jeep, wearing the same clothing and with his French Polish boots. He gave us a weak smile as we passed, but a week later he was removed from command. The Second-in-Command was made Commanding Officer and not before time.

Further on we passed a group of squaddies digging latrines for Battalion Headquarters. Private Beetroot was among them and he gave us a cheery wave. Looking at the others in the squad, I saw they were all from different companies and all looked downcast and ashamed. They had been removed from the line for the same reason. "Lack of Moral Fibre". For me though, the biggest shock of all was the Corporal in Charge. He had been in the same Platoon as me in Germany. He was a Geordie who had worked in the mines all through the war. He was unable to leave his restricted trade but, as soon as the war was over, he had joined the Army. By nature he was a very loud mouthed extrovert who always had to be on top in any situation and was crude and boastful. I had a chat with him and asked what he was doing there. "It was those shells!" he said. In short, he was there for the same reason as all the others. He just could not take it. I learned a lot about Social Behaviour that day.

We now had a period of seven days in a sort of rest camp some miles behind the lines. Mind you, a rest was all it was. We had no films, shows or concert parties, although 29 Brigade had the benefit of these. We of 27 Brigade were the forgotten army. Thrown into battle in a rush as a stop gap and to be forgotten as soon as possible. This was the same attitude that prevailed throughout our time in Korea. We did have two sing-along parties but these were of our own making. A drinking party was organised by someone in a Korean cottage, but only about one third of the men could attend. There was a limited amount of beer available, but Sgt. Swede gave me a bottle of gin he had obtained from the Sergeants' Mess. So unused were we to alcohol that a little went a long way. After an hour or so of singing and boasting, I went outside to the urinal, (a heap of stones), and was happily relieving myself when I found myself lying face down. I rejoined the party but not for long. I went to my tent where Pte. Sprout was sleeping. I awoke in the morning with a God Almighty hangover. I was not cured of party going though. Three days later, I was invited to another party where most of the guests were men from all the other companies as well as Battalion Headquarters. I was accompanied by a National Service Corporal from my Platoon. He was a prospect for University and a very nice chap.

The party went well but Cpl. University and I decided we had enjoyed ourselves enough and staggered on our merry way to bed. Suddenly, I felt a blow on my brow just above the left eye. As I lay on the ground, I saw Cpl. University surrounded by three others who were laying into him. "All right!" he cried out. "I'm going!" We two got back to our tents where I was put to bed by faithful Sprout. I was crying my eyes out. Later I learnt that some dregs of the Regiment had stolen a crate of beer from the Sergeants' Mess and were waiting for the two Corporals to get out of the way. Apparently, we were not moving fast enough and it was decided to hurry us along. I still have the scar.

On what proved to be the last day of rest, we heard the news of the Gloucestershire Regiment on the River Imjin. The event is well known by now but it gave us an awful shock. The Argyle and Sutherland Highlanders, our sister regiment, were already at Pusan awaiting to embark and were allowed to proceed. We of the Middlesex were told, "Pack your kit. You are going back up the line."

During our last couple of weeks in Korea, we at first did the usual of wandering up hill and down dale, but for the last week or so we were holding a fixed position on the line which by now had been firmly established. Before this though, we had one peculiar experience. We marched to where the New Zealand gunners, with their 25 Pounders, were in daily and nightly operation. All the Corporals and Below were bedded down at a distance of two hundred yards in front of the muzzles and told we were the Gunners' defence in case of attack. This sounded fair enough but then came the dusk. We were asleep and then the Guns opened up. The muzzle velocity of the shells made an enormous noise which almost burst our ear drums. The first salvo was a huge shock to our system and, to our way of thinking, was entirely unnecessary. Salvo after salvo was blasted off during the night and we had no pleasure at all in knowing it was directed at the enemy. Quite why we were put in this position I have no idea. Just a bit of a joke I rather fancy.

By this time we had a new Platoon Commander, a National Service 2/Lt. who relied heavily on advice from Sgt. Swede. This advice was not always the most learned or the wisest. The first operation in which 2/Lt. Gooseberry was involved was an advance over a couple of hills which were supposedly occupied by the enemy. If they were there it was in very small numbers. We formed up at the base of the first hill and, as usual, I was given the order to lead the way. I started off and for the very first time I found I just did not want to go up this hill. I went very slowly and half way up 2/Lt. Gooseberry and Sgt. Swede drew level with me. They both looked at me with some curiosity but I was past caring. For seven months I had led every advance and taken out every patrol bar one. I did not mind being an equal partner in time of danger, but every single time it was me and me alone who was out in front. As I was soon to discover, my section also had thought about our position in the Company and indeed in the battalion.

Having reached the top of the first hill we took a rest. Facing us was another hill but connected by a gentle slope in between. The other hill had a plateau on the left and a sharp peak on the right which supposedly hid the enemy. 2/Lt. Gooseberry and Sgt. Swede were having a conference and within minutes I was called over. I was given the usual orders to lead the way to the plateau. I went back to the section to give them the tidings. To my surprise and mortification the section called me every name under the sun. I sat down and was nearly in tears, although the whole platoon knew the abuse was really directed at the Platoon Commander. He looked dismayed but called upon another section to lead the advance. The second section followed and I trailed along behind. I was humiliated by the mutiny but the lads had every justification for their actions. We were all near breaking point but my section were fed up to the back teeth with being first, first and first again. Any feeling of honour had long since vanished.

The advance over the plateau invoked no response from the enemy, although the senior officers were convinced that the Chinese were in position on the peak. We went to the far side of the plateau and were ordered to rest just below the crest. We had a grandstand view of the enemy, about half a mile away, being plastered with artillery fire and rockets from the Sabre jets. We had to start a fire to heat up our cans of food but the ground was bare of fuel. We had passed just one solitary fir tree on the way and I reasoned there could be some twigs lying around. I went back on my own and I was right about the twigs although they were very tiny. I was entirely alone on the plateau and only 100 yards from the peak. Because the first hill was much lower than the plateau, I was in full view of the rest of my battalion and also of the Australians on the right of the line.

I started collecting up the twigs in my cap comforter being very anxious to please my lads who were still in a state of mutiny, but very loyal to me. I hadn't been going for long when I heard the sound of a mortar bomb descending. I threw myself flat and the bomb exploded not ten yards from where I was lying. I stood up and saw the shallow crater was made by a three inch mortar and what's more it came from either my own regiment or the Australians. I put it down to some fluke shot and carried on gathering twigs. After all, my Company had been seen going over the hill and the plateau and were now out of sight. A lone figure had come back dressed only in combat gear and without arms or equipment. Then I heard another bomb descending and threw myself flat in the first crater – this on the age old principle that shells never land in the same place twice. I carried on searching for twigs and kept throwing myself down in the last crater. This went on for bombs three, four, five, six, seven, eight, nine and ten. When I stood up after bomb number seven, I noticed that bomb number six had landed on the crater of number four.

It was blindingly obvious to me after bomb number three that I was the target and what's more the mortar crew were fantastically accurate. I should have been long gone but I was very stubborn. I had to collect that fuel. I now had a cap full of twigs and started back towards the Company. Just then Private Sprout came towards me and asked what was going on. I mumbled something about being mistaken for the enemy and we went back to the section. The lads had managed to get a fire gong but my contribution was extremely welcome. The mortar episode was never mentioned again by anybody. I have thought long and hard about it and conclude it was the Australians who had used me for target practise. Although the blast of each explosion had wafted over my body, I never suffered a scratch. The Aussies must have been furious to see me walk away.

After a meal, we were ordered to go down a dry river bed and on the enemy's side of the hill. We had not gone very far when the Company was halted, without any indication of how long. We were standing on pebbles which yielded to our feet and looked and felt deliciously soft. We kept our equipment on but lay on our backs with our small packs hitched up to form a pillow. It was heaven. As a minor matter, I for one noticed that the Yank artillery were firing air bursts − shells designed to explode in the air and spread shrapnel over a large area.

I was feeling dozy when I felt a blow on my shoulder. It wasn't hard but I knew it was from a pebble. I ignored the incident but then had another pebble hit my head. I was furious! What idiot had the strength to play such a childish game! I turned over on my stomach and looked around for the culprit. Just then I saw the pebbles near my face move and jump all of their own accord. I wasn't hit by a pebble this time but I realised the cause of the pebbles moving about. It was shrapnel from the air bursts. I looked at my sleeping partners but nobody moved a muscle. I was the sole recipient of the near misses. Of course, my first instinct was to run for cover but there was no cover whatsoever. To move at all was only to run into danger. I turned on my back and went to sleep. It was one of those dangerous moments when I could do nothing about the situation.

CHAPTER THIRTY

Dishonourable Conduct

Throughout the age of warfare it has always been the tendency to blame the enemy for acts of a very nasty nature and moments of uncivilised behaviour. Naturally, no regiment will recall or write about such incidents, but I feel I must ignore this principal for the sake of truth.

On about the sixth day of the battle of Billingsgate, when hostilities had ceased for the time being, a Corporal came into view from the direction of Headquarters. He was in his early forties and carried nothing but a pair of pliers. The Corporal was followed by a simpleton of a lad grinning inanely as he followed his hero. The Corporal also appeared to be under the influence of drink. The simpleton told us that they were on their way to extract the gold teeth from the Chinese corpses. We were only faintly disgusted, but also curious. How did the Corporal know about the gold teeth? It was one thing to kill the enemy, but to mess about with the bodies was another. Of course, it was our duty to search for documents and such like but, after that, the corpses were ignored as far as possible. The two of them went on their way to where the bodies were known to have been but the dugouts were now in possession of the Aussies. Ten minutes later the grave robbers returned looking very downcast. There was no need of any explanation.

The Aussies had put them in their place and probably with some choice language.

I was still curious though about the gold teeth. In my childhood in the 1930s there was always somebody to be seen flashing a gold tooth or two. They were especially favoured by the rather nastier inhabitants of Great Britain, but not unknown to the more decent middle classes. I myself have no idea of how these teeth were constructed. Were they solid teeth or real teeth with the gold plated on? It is still a mystery to me but the vanity of gold teeth had great appeal in the Far East. Consequently, many an Asian corpse displayed flashing molars. The real question though — is the value of the gold worth the extraction? If my curiosity was aroused it was never satisfied after Billingsgate as I never saw another corpse.

But to get on. By now late April, it had been decided that the war would be continued by having the two armies facing each other from a fixed position behind barbed wire. My regiment was concerned only with the very early stages of this type of warfare but which continued for another two years. Our ridge was not all that high, but we were not the first up at that position. The barbed wire was already in place. Coils of it had been spread just below the crest but a trifle too high up in my humble opinion! Each Company platoon and section were allocated a stretch of the path which ran along the ridge for a mile or more. We now had to dig slit trenches along the path with sleeping areas to the rear. Although we never saw the Chinese and were never troubled by them, they were in some hills about a mile away across a flat valley of paddy fields.

On our left were the King's Own Scottish Borders and on our right were the Americans. My platoon was on the extreme right of the British forces and so we were slap up against the

Yanks. And what a contrast! We British, as per our training and from sheer common sense, dug our trenches just below the crest and on the rear slope. The Yanks dug their trenches on the forward slope. This meant that small arms fire could be directed straight into the trench system. Even if the British had to dig in on the crest, we at least had several feet of earth or rock to assist in our protection. There was one other difference between us and the Yanks. When we dug a trench it was meant for two men and each trench was next to another. In other words, the defence was just a single line of men. The Yanks not only dug in on the forward slope, but they had several lines of trenches going from top to bottom . Whether this was more effective we never found out. Incidentally, the Yanks had no barbed wire in front of them – a major defect in any fixed position.

We British, of course, never fired our weapons unless we had specific orders to do so. Sentries were instructed to use their common sense as sometimes the enemy merely made a noise to find out where the sentries were positioned. Except in the case of my own two berks! I never knew anybody to open fire "just in case". The GIs on the other hand fired as and where they felt like it. Each time a sentry was changed over, the newcomer would invariably lose off a few rounds at a suspicious bush. This went on right through the day as well as the night. "I thought I saw something!" was the usual excuse. Each Yank was also at liberty to leave his trench at the slightest whim and so there was a constant coming and going. The Chinese not only knew where each trench was situated, but must have known the exact number of bodies in opposition!

During this last two weeks of being in the line, we never had a single missile of any sort sent our way. Not a shell, mortar bomb or bullet. Just as well as there were no longer any war horses left among us. No champing at the bit to pull the guns towards the heathen savages or the Boers or the vile Hun. Any writer for the Boys' Own Paper would have found little inspiration among the Regiment at that time. Not that there was no military activity at all. Half way through this quiet time, it was decided to send out a patrol in the direction of the foe. Now the entire fighting element of the battalion was on that ridge and the command of the last patrol of our war should have been regarded as something of an honour.

A number of reinforcement subalterns had never actually heard a shot fired in anger or, at least, only from a distance. When word was spread among Headquarters about the patrol, there should have been a clamour of volunteers for the privilege of command. But no! Word came down the line from Battalion to Company to Platoon and I was nominated as the Patrol Leader. Humble Corporal Cabbage. I was given instructions that I was to go forward for one hour, pause and return. Now the normal walking pace for a soldier was three miles an hour, but nobody expected me to walk straight on as though on a route march. That would be rather silly. I was given a compass and told that the King's Own Scottish Borderers would be sending out a patrol at the same time. That rather worried me. I would have rather have been on my own as any bodies sighted would be the enemy. I was also very, very concerned about the Yanks on my right. A continuous Guy Fawkes celebration was one thing, but their bullets were not confined to the ground immediately to their front. Many shots strayed left to the area in front of my Company.

While it was still daylight, I took a look at the area to my front and visualised a straight line leading from the right hand side of the K.O.S.B. position towards the Chinese. I visualised another line from the left hand side of the Yanks. The resulting square was with me at the south and the Chinese at the north. At a point midway between north west and north east, I selected a hill on which I could take a compass bearing. Let's say it was 350 degrees. I rotated the top dial until the movable arrow was set at 350 degrees and resolved to follow that bearing without any deviation. I had no need to take a note of the reverse bearing as I would have an excellent beacon to show me the way home.

Choosing three of my men, we set off at 11pm. A gap had been left in the wire where we could walk through and down the forward slope. We carried no equipment, only weapons and a minimal amount of ammo. I led the way and we went forward at a cautious pace, pausing now and then to listen. After an hour, shown by my ever precious watch, we stopped and spread out to keep all round observation. It was a still night and with a fair amount of light. I reckoned we had travelled about three quarters of a mile, but we were still some distance from the Chinese. I turned over on my side and, resting on one elbow, I looked back. The view was fantastic. The ridge occupied by The Middlesex and the K.O.S.B.'s was jet black against the night sky. Not the faintest indication of a light. The part occupied by the GIs was a blaze of light from one end to another where the ridge curled around towards the rear.

There were scores of flashing lights from torches and even fires in front of the trench. Now and then a light would go out for a second as someone walked in front of it. There was also a murmur of constant sound and we could even catch a shout or two. There were the tiny flashes of light from the muzzles of guns and the whole panorama went on without ceasing for a moment. I signalled to my men and we went back but still with a lot of caution. It was those casual shots from the Yanks that was our worst worry. I approached the gap in the wire and heard "Halt!" and the first part of the password. I replied with the second part and we went on through the gap. For the first time ever there was someone waiting to get my report. We got bedded down for the remainder of the night.

That was the one and only patrol sent out from the ridge by my regiment. In real terms, for that type of warfare, there should have been a patrol sent out every night if not two or maybe three. If there was any honour to be gained from commanding the last patrol, I did not even get a verbal "Well done!"

The weather now was quite nice and even sunny. We had recently got rid of our American Combat Jacket and Trousers but there was no question of merely throwing it away. Each Platoon was lined up and the Colour Sergeant solemnly ticked off the list as the items were thrown into the back of a truck. These garments had been worn night and day for eight months in all kinds of conditions. What did the regiment do with this stuff? Sell it back to the Yanks? Our headgear had been thrown away by this time. They were rather warm and uncomfortable come March. I had started the vogue when I took my cap comforter from around my neck, where it was a scarf, and folded it into a cap as worn by our Commandos in World War Two. Within two days every officer and man were wearing their Commando cap.

On one particular sunny day, I left the position and went down the slope to a grassy spot. I took off my battledress and boots and lay in the sun for half an hour. My legs were bare from the top of my socks to the bottom of my summer shorts. (The woollen vest and long johns had also gone.) I got dressed with a sigh of relief but twenty four hours later I knew I was well and truly sunburnt. It was agony but at least my knees were already brown when we got to Hong Kong.

There was one other pleasing aspect about that ridge, and that was the food. We had to go down to where a cookhouse (in a large marquee) had been established and collect our food in our mess tins. We ate it on the grass and I must say it was superb. How the cooks managed in such conditions with those petrol burning stoves, I have no idea, but we really felt spoilt. And it wasn't because it was such a change from the U.S. 'C' rations.

CHAPTER THIRTY ONE

The Last Two Weeks

This last chapter is made up of a mish mash of stories, but all of them equally important in their own right and each one helps to explain the whole picture.

For instance, there were always some senior officers and senior NCOs who liked to compare the Korean War with other campaigns such as the Desert of Normandy or Burma. They used expressions like :- "Now the conditions in North Africa were really tough. Hardly any water and the flies were unbelievable." After the first couple of months these comparisons died a merciful death and for a very good reason. The Korean War had no comparison with any other war fought by the British Army. It was so, so different I myself cannot detail the differences even though I was a very active participant. After just a few months, we all knew it was different from any other campaign, and for one reason only. We never knew what was coming next!

A typical example of misinformation was given to me by a Corporal of the King's Own Shropshire Infantry. This regiment took over from us in May 1951 and, incidentally, this really was our last day in the line. Anyway, this rather obnoxious personality had been detailed to take over my section of the line. I first explained our arcs of fire. When an infantry section first set up a system of trenches, the Platoon Commander goes around and details how far left and right the Bren gunner can traverse this weapon. This ensures that all three Bren guns are not concentrated on one spot, leaving part of the enemy position uncovered.

Now, of course, my Platoon Commander had not detailed the arcs of fire. I rather doubt if he knew what the expression meant. He was after all a National Serviceman and had not had time to absorb every facet of the Infantry Manual. Anyway, I had picked out my own arcs of fire and I explained them to the Corporal. He in turn did not seem all that interested in such mundane matters, but was very anxious to ask about something else. Eventually he spoke out. "Tell me! What does the enemy soldier look like when he comes charging towards you with bayonet fixed and screaming his head off?"

The war had been going on now for eleven months with daily doses of news items in every newspaper in the world, together with lurid descriptions by the participants and the survivors; and there was no need for embellishment – the simple truth was all too real for those in the thick of it. The Corporal had obviously been reading up on the war, and there was no reason to think he had been misled, but now he was asking for my experience. In the one second I had left to answer, I thought of all the possible situations that I could use for a reply. First, there was the North Korean who had stood up to surrender but he was not the answer. He never charged towards us. There were also the two teams of machine gunners who charged over the hill, but I was looking at them through binoculars so I could not really count them. There was a pair of eyes looking over a sub-machine gun while he fired at me. There was the sniper who fired at me many times but all I saw of him was an arm and a rifle. He would not do either. There were the grenade throwers only yards away but, in spite of the obvious dangers, none of them could fit the description wanted.

At the end of my reflections, I simply told the truth. "I don't know," I said. "I've never seen one standing up!" The Corporal looked at me with an expression of utter contempt and walked away. I have wondered ever since if he ever saw his "enemy soldier charging towards him with bayonet fixed" and what he felt about it at the time.

I have tried to explain that we carried an enormous weight of equipment at all times in Korea as there was a tendency to hold on to everything "just in case." The items carried included two .36 grenades. These weighed a pound and a half each. Before we went up the last ridge, we were given another four grenades each. I at least had a problem finding somewhere to put them. Every nook and cranny was already full up. Eventually I succeeded somehow, but another six pounds was almost the last straw! When we got to the top of that last ridge, I threw off the equipment with relief. A couple of minutes was taken up with instructions as to where my section slit trenches would be, and I then bent down to pick up my equipment with one hand. I could not budge it.

I ask the reader to imagine, if not actually try, a large suitcase being gradually filled with bricks until it can no longer be lifted with one hand. That's the way it was with me. I felt embarrassed but I don't know why. I lifted up my belt and pouches first and fitted them on my body. Then I lifted up my pack and slung it over my shoulder. Only then could I move. When I put them down again, it was with great relief. Never again would I carry all that weight as we left behind the six grenades and some ammo. By the way, a large number of those grenades recently issued never went up the hill. They went down a nearby well! A check was never made by the Platoon Officers and I thought the dumping of the grenades was rather silly under the circumstances, but the culprits got away with their deception.

A little habit I acquired in Korea was one I call "looking out of the window." I suppose most of us, upon entering a room which is empty, take a glance out of the window. I do it all the time, although I know perfectly well what I will see. In Korea it was a precautionary measure. Although we always had sentries posted, I would persistently take a look over the top towards the enemy. Even when moving from one position to another, and below the ridge, I would always climb up a couple of steps to have a look. It was a habit so ingrained that if we happened to be miles from the front, I habitually looked north whenever I got to my feet, or even when on the march. Never south.

Although I was unaware of my mental condition at the time, I now realise that I was on the verge of a breakdown towards the end and, indeed, so were the rest of the battalion. When we got back to Hong Kong, it was of the opinion of the Medical Authorities that the whole regiment were "bomb happy" and how right they were! The average citizen is under the impression that Combat Fatigue is caused purely by the weight of shot and shell thrown at the soldier, but this is only part of the story. The stress of command is a very big factor in breakdowns. Why else would a Brigadier collapse when he had already proved his personal courage? My own C.O. collapsed after being awarded the Distinguished Service Order. My third Company Commander gave in when he came under fire for the very first time in Korea. My Platoon Commander did quite well in our first fire fight, but thereafter deteriorated until he had to be evacuated.

For most, especially for private soldiers, it is the waiting that can create havoc on the mind. The fear of the great uncertainty. For myself, I was invariably glad to be in a fire fight. The clouds of depression lifted and I was in my element. I was doing what I was paid for and I did not have to pretend. That is not to say I was never afraid, but my worst moments came from friendly fire. Twice shelled by the Canadians, once by the Americans, and mortared by the Australians. I still never gave in, but I was horrified by the thought of being hit by my comrades. It did something to my nervous system which I can never explain.

Going forward again to Hong Kong – there were a few incidents that related to the Korean War that surprised me at least. The first relates to the cooks who produced such terrific food under very harsh conditions. Those same cooks now produced meals that were plainly awful. Even the Christmas cake was made with dehydrated potato instead of flour. The cooks had many excuses, but I rather think the rations were being flogged to the Chinese – which means the Catering Officer was a disgrace.

In another incident, a subaltern came to me and said, "We simply must do something about the Company Sergeant Major! The poor chap can't go on any longer." I for one had no idea that there was anything wrong with him. In Korea, the C.S.M. was the least seen person in the Company. Not that it was his fault. His duties required him to organise the Company Headquarters and, in doing just that, a bit too much was left on his shoulders. Anyway, there was nothing I could do but I did wonder why we hardly saw anything of him in Hong Kong. Back in peace time barracks, the C.S.M. would be everywhere and into everything. Here in Hong Kong, he was present in name only. Anyway, he was sent home shortly after, but for the life of me I can't remember anyone taking his place. I did rather think at the time, "Why can't we all go home?"

In yet another post script to Korea, I was very surprised one day when Private Sprout said to me, "I never fired my rifle in Korea." I had actually noticed at one time when I had given my lads the order to open fire that Sprout had never responded, but I had forgotten all about it. There had been a couple of incidents earlier when my section were required to open fire, but I never thought I actually had to check they were doing so. When troops are under small army fire and they can't run away, the usual response would be to return the fire to ensure their own safety. At least that was my way of thinking. Apparently I was in a minority. Lt. Plum was a prime example of fear overcoming reason. With grenades exploding ever nearer, Plum just lay there hoping that something – **anything** – would save him. Sgt. Swede and the rest of the platoon followed suit.

When Sprout had made his remark, another lad said, "I never fired mine either!" He wasn't one of my chaps, but I had no doubt he was telling the truth. On reflection, I rather think there were quite a number in the company who had kept their weapons clean. The mentality here is, "If I don't fire at him he won't fire at me!" but when the enemy has actually opened fire, this reasoning should go by the board. I did notice though that where troops have opened fire for the first time, they then become very enthusiastic. If only Sprout had fired his rifle during that first week in Korea.

If only Lt. Plum had given his platoon the order to fire when we were watching the U.S. tank taking on the North Korean tank in that first week, he may have been a different man. Mind you, the reluctance to give the order to open fire was endemic in the battalion and I believe the reason for this was instructions from on high to avoid casualties because of the large contingent of National Servicemen within our ranks. Anything to appease the wrath of the British Public who would turn on the Military without hesitation.

It is a pity that the old maxim, "The best form of defence is attack" was not more widely known among our back seat drivers.

One outstanding feature of the British Korean War was the adamant refusal to admit the existence of Combat Fatigue. When it was first realised during the First World War that shell shock was a genuine battle illness, it was still largely covered up. During World War Two there was a more enlightened recognition of the effects of Combat but in Korea it was not acknowledged at all. The British from the start had been led to believe that the Korean War was just a little local difficulty which would soon be cleaned up. The admission of Combat Fatigue within the first few months would show that conditions were far worse than the Brass Hats had allowed for – and so the cover up. The old excuse, "If we let one get away with it, they will **all** be at it!" was fully exercised at all levels.

Thinking back, I recognise that we had four enemies in Korea and they were The North Koreans, The Chinese, Combat Fatigue and, in my regiment, the fourth was our Quartermaster.

Now in a peace time barracks the pressure on the Quartermaster to conserve clothing, equipment and rations was enormous. If, for instance, the allowance for replacement socks was one thousand pairs of socks among one thousand men, then it must not be one thousand and one. Otherwise the Civil Servants back in Britain would create an almighty uproar. In a war, however, there was opportunity to write off all sorts of stores as lost "due to enemy action" but not with our Quartermaster. Everything went by the book – the peace time book, that is.

Mind you, when we had a parade to issue vests and socks and underpants, then the kit was issued without question. Otherwise, there was no "out of hours" replacement. On one disastrous day I had my large pack stolen by the Australians. The large packs were kept on the Company truck and we had access to them on only a few occasions. They contained spare shirts and stuff like that.

The first thing I had to replace was the large pack and this took a lot of argument. Gradually I replaced the other items, but some not until we were in Hong Kong. The fact that we had men killed and wounded and shell shocked in many shoot outs made no impression on our Quartermaster. None whatsoever! Every man was expected to have the full quota of equipment, but not one item more. This reasoning made us suffice with one pair of woollen gloves which were wholly inadequate at twenty five below zero, but we were never supplied with another pair.

Like the time that we had to hand in our American combat clothing. The jacket and trousers had been worn for twenty-four hours a day, awake or asleep, rain, snow or sun, and in every degree of filth and contact with dead bodies. I did rather fancy keeping my jacket but I knew what we would be carrying back to Hong Kong and I had to stifle my desire. In any case, the Colour Sergeant carefully listed every man as the clothing was thrown in the back of the truck. Now what happened to that stuff? Was it sold back to the Yanks?

All in all, the Regiment did a pretty good job in Korea but with very little appreciation from the top brass. After all, we had been the basis of considerable embarrassment for the British Government. Time and again we had survived some very hot spots despite every attempt to keep us away from trouble altogether. After Korea, I made a mental count of the number of days in which I had been under fire and it came to twenty one. I made no distinction between enemy or friendly fire, nor between shell fire or just one or two bullets. It's all dangerous stuff!

A total of fifteen members of the regiment received gallantry awards ranging from the Distinguished Service Order to a Mention in Dispatches. Two members received two awards each. Four of the awards were American. My Company 'C' were awarded nothing at all. This is not surprising as we lost a Major to a stupid accident, and another Major and a Subaltern to shell shock amidst the fighting. Another subaltern was mortally wounded in rather suspicious circumstances. Twice my Company had been sent forward to engage the enemy and twice had been withdrawn through lack of leadership.

There was only the one death in 'C' Company and in my own section there were no casualties at all, unless you count the deserter. The battalion are listed as having ninety four wounded, but I am willing to bet that does not include the shell shock cases. My own Platoon Commander was mentioned as being concussed rather than given the real reason for his removal from the line.

As a finale to this saga, I must bring the Quartermaster's staff into our final moments of the War. We were all lined up alongside a river to be issued with a new blue beret. There were several tables heaped with berets of various sizes. The

Regimental Quarter Master Sergeant reigned supreme. He was in a very jovial mood and was using expressions of mateyness. I tried to make sense of his attitude and, in the end, put it down to guilt. I thought of all the little extras we could have received and didn't. Not a morsel of food over the ration. Not a single pair of socks or gloves over the allotted span. No picture shows or other entertainment. Not that the R.Q.M.S. was solely to blame for all this, but he was there in full sight – a handy culprit.

Anyway, my turn came. The R.Q.M.S. had set himself as an expert on head sizes and was using expressions like, "Now! You're a size six and seven eighths. I can always tell!"

To me he said, "You're a size seven. Try this on!"

I replied, "No, Sir! I'm a seven and one eighth..."

"No, you're not! You're a size seven." I tried on the size seven and it was too tight.

The R.Q.M.S.'s face darkened and he threw at me a size seven and one eighth with the words...

"There's always one troublemaker!"

~ END ~

Recruit training, May 1945 – author in front row, 4th from left.

On the 7th day of the battle of Billingsgate

The last fag of the day.

Two months since our last bath.

A very temporary clubhouse in North Korea.

A mortally wounded lieutenant in brought in.

A day in the line in the winter mud, snow and cold.

Goodbye to the front – waiting for the train to take me home, 1951.